Wife Mistress Slave
Position Passion Submission

Wife Mistress Slave

Position Passion Submission

Insight and Practical Advice
for Husbands, Wives and the other Woman

Dominic Valentine

To order additional copies of this book, contact:
Xlibris Corporation
1-888-795-4274
www.Xlibris.com
Orders@Xlibris.com
37711

CONTENTS

Dedicated

To
My wife
For
These inspiring words

Don't let anyone make decisions in what YOU believe in, in what YOU want and need in your life. You have rare qualities. When a man has all of these qualities rolled up into his mind, body, and soul he can conquer the world, that's YOU in every sense. You will never let anyone or anything get you down or take your spirit away; that's what keeps you high. Keep being you, continue to express your feelings without feeling guilty, continue to enjoy life with anyone you want to enjoy life with, do what MAKES you HAPPY. Do what you want to do FOR YOU and ONLY YOU. You can do this because you have such a caring, warm, passionate love for mankind. You have the Strength, the Courage, and the Pride that makes you who you are. Take care of yourself for us.

Your Number One Fan, I Love You,

FOREWORD

I am a wife, happily married for over 30 years to a wonderful man. Together we have built a home, a business and a family.

I've been a mistress in a wild passionate love affair, the kind that is written in the stars and very few are fortunate enough to experience.

I am a slave to a wonderful Master. He is my friend and mentor as well. Ours is a unique relationship, but one I wouldn't trade for another.

I've held many different positions in my life and still do. Women are used to juggling and multi-tasking in our day-to-day lives and we all have a closet full of the many different hats we have worn, and will wear, in our lifetime.

This book is about different women and their various positions in, and throughout, life. Some positions we create for ourselves, some are created by others and some come from our heart. Those that come from our heart are truly who and what we are. We may try different positions, perhaps to find ourselves or perhaps just for the experience. Yet in full circle, we always come back to our heart.

Accepting my position in life as a slave wasn't easy for me. I fought it and I fought him. He taught me things and made me look inside of myself to see what was really there. But while I know and have lived these different positions, sometimes reading what you've always felt makes it all come together.

What struck me the hardest, was reading about me. Even though I've lived what Valentine has written, I never understood any of it. Reading his words put it in perspective and it has allowed me to find peace in my personal situation.

Funny thing is, I thought I had found that peace once before. It lasted for a while until that ugly head of unreasoning arose once again. After reading *Wife Mistress Slave*, I understood and accepted the changes.

I know a great number of women will read this book and be put out by it; offended by it. Their first instinct will be to throw it away.

Please don't. Read it in its entirety. Read it with an open mind, but most of all, read it with an open heart. You may see yourself in it more than once; perhaps a similar situation, perhaps a similar thought. This book will help you understand what it was you felt or thought. And it will help you understand some of the dark thoughts you most likely still harbor today.

I know. I went through those dark thoughts. I questioned everything and never understood anything. Sometimes, I still don't understand, but I have learned to accept that everyone is different.

Whatever position you choose to be for the man in your life, you cannot give it your all until you have found peace within yourself. By finding yourself, you will find peace. Be happy with yourself. Embrace your chosen position. Embrace the man in your life. Show the world your strength. Share your happiness and embrace others with your love.

His Sweet Slave

CHAPTER 1

WHY WRITE THIS BOOK?

This question begs asking almost as much as the question of why anyone would buy this book. What purpose is served by writing a book on a subject so taboo that very few speak honestly on it? After all, the reality is that few women will ever admit to sharing the man they love with another woman. Oh sure, the average woman can participate in ménage a trois within her lifetime or even date a married man once or twice, but to actually knowingly and purposely share her man on an ongoing basis is practically unheard of.

I'm not here to convince anyone that the pluralistic lifestyle is superior or even equal to the monogamous lifestyle. In fact, studies usually show the contrary. Yet the fact remains that, even with all the reasons that a man may have to be monogamous, his nature is pluralistic.

I started to write this book to outline protocol and etiquette for all parties involved in my pluralistic lifestyle. This included my wife, my mistress, my sex slave, my platonic female friends and, of course, me.

Though this is why I originally started to write the book I slowly changed what I hope the reader will gain from it. I found that the information contained in my manuscript could possibly give a better understanding of man's desire to consummate more than one relationship at a time.

Even though I believe it impossible for one woman to be a wife, mistress and slave, I came to the conclusion that women will never quit trying in hopes of keeping their men from seeking, and participating in, outside relationships.

To that I can only say, "Bravo!" I now understand that, just as I should always have the right to desire and participate in plural relationships, so should every woman have the same right to desire and participate in a monogamous relationship. If reading this book helps any woman achieve a monogamous relationship by giving her new insight and alternatives, then I have truly done a wonderful thing. I say this, because I know from personal experience that no man stays monogamous because he is forced to but rather because he wants to.

A HISTORICAL PERSPECTIVE

I'm one of very few men who admit that he is polygamous by nature and has spent his whole adult life openly desiring or participating in poly relationships.

In the beginning, I searched for a lifestyle in which I could have multiple women in the same household. In short, I was looking for an open polygamous type of lifestyle. I understood the law and knew that I could not legally marry more than one woman, but I did envision myself living in a household with multiple women whom I saw as my wives. Today these relationships are known as polyamorous rather than polygamous, because there are not multiple marriages, but rather multiple loving and committed relationships.

I entered into my first open poly relationship when I was 18 and have for the most part openly embraced this lifestyle for 30 years. It was only for a short period during the rearing of my children that I did not openly seek out, or participate in, poly relationships, but the desire was always there.

When my children grew up, I once again embraced the desire for this lifestyle. After 30 years, I have come to the conclusion that polygamous/polyamorous relationships very rarely work. It's not for the reason of jealousy, but rather the lack of a social environment that supports them. This is why most polygamous communities tend to stay very secluded, free of most outside influence.

What I found that worked—and continues to work in western society—are plural relationships. Instead of the man being involved in open loving relationships with multiple women, he chooses to take on outside relationships that are either hidden from, or ignored by, his wife. It is these pluralistic relationships, not poly relationships, which are the subject of this book.

My writings are neither my attempt to justify nor rationalize plural relationships or extramarital affairs. On the contrary, these activities have gone on since the dawn of man and nothing short of the destruction of mankind will stop them. They do not need my justification.

This book is not meant to encourage men and women to participate in plural relationships. It is merely a conveyance of knowledge that very few possess about why men desire multiple relationships and where they fail. This book is a guide for men and women who have accepted that they are, and will continue to be, involved in a plural relationship or with a partner that has pluralistic desires. And even though I don't like to give false hope that one woman can be every type of woman in a man's life, I do believe this book can serve as a guide for the women who want to make an honest attempt.

Finally, I would hope that this book identifies and spotlights the stupid and selfish things that men do that compound the pain women feel when they knowingly or unknowingly are involved in a plural relationship.

I am not the only man to desire a poly lifestyle, but by doing so openly I have been able to get feedback from men and women that has fueled continued analysis of this socially expected (but not socially accepted) act of plural relationships for men. We all know it's going on but we all act like we don't.

It was while viewing a DVD of the ShowTime Original movie *Feast of All Saints* that I realized what I had been searching for, why I had been searching and why I had never been able to successfully maintain it. The original book, written by Anne Rice, chronicles the plight of the women of color who migrated to New Orleans during the early 1800's from a revolution-torn Haiti.

These women of color were not slaves, but rather free Creole people of French and African heritage. They were considered bourgeoisie and very desirable by Black and White men, alike. Many of these exotic beauties became the mistresses of wealthy plantation owners and business men of Louisiana in a ritual known as placage. Contracts, signed by the men, mandatory in many cases, guaranteed their mistress a minimum standard of living and provided for their care and the care of offspring arising from these relationships. The mistresses were also given servants/slaves for their use, but not for their ownership. These slaves belonged to the man who used them in whatever capacity he saw fit, up to and including sexually.

Let's recap. The gentleman had his wife at his primary home, his mistress at his secondary residence and slaves at both. In horse racing, I believe, this would be known as the trifecta, first second and third place.

In first place was the wife, who was chosen to help the family acquire and maintain wealth. She was also chosen for the position her family held within a certain social-economic circle. Therefore this marriage supported if not elevated the man's status within that same circle. Although the marriage was a loveless one it did suffice in providing the man with the proper woman to hold the position of wife.

In second place was the mistress and the relationship was quite passionate. The sex was so erotically charged that, even upon returning home to the plantation, he found himself thinking of being back in the city with her. This beauty provided the passion in his life.

Finally, in third place was the slave. She was his property, to do with as he pleased. If the man enjoyed any type of fetish, then he could express it with her. He held the power of her life and death in his hands. When called upon, this bonded woman took care of all the domestic as well as sexual duties. She was his property and this type of relationship gives any man a king-like, if not God-like, complex.

Out of this revelation came my understanding of the wife, mistress and slave. I suddenly understood why successful men craved it, indeed needed it to feel complete as men. Here was a man who had all three and each knew her place within his life. He could have maintained this arrangement indefinitely had he remembered two simple rules. Rule #1: respect and value each woman for the position that she holds in your life. And rule #2: never give the impression that any of them will ever hold any other place in your life.

So there you have it, position of the wife, passion of the mistress, submission of a slave, every powerful man's dream and many a powerful man's reality

As you go forward, please remember that these are the opinions of one man, but nonetheless, opinions formulated over a 30-year period of self-study and the study of plural relationships. I have also found, within my studies, that many successful men today desire this same lifestyle, so common 200 years ago. Unfortunately, for 21st Century gentlemen, it is a general belief that one woman should be able to fulfill all of these needs, even though it is unlikely in reality.

THE SUBJECT ITSELF

Polygamy, adultery, sado-masochism and slavery are adult subjects and, as such, need to be taken very seriously.

It is said that the crime of rape is not about sex, but about control and power. I submit that the driving force in a man's desire for multiple relationships is also not about sex, but rather about power. I also submit that it is the average woman's attraction to powerful men, which fuels this desire.

The men that I'm referring to in this book are what I considered successful men. In this particular case, I determine their success partially by their education (formal and informal) and partially by their economic status. Economic and educational statuses often indicate a man's ability to apply energy and turn it into power.

The men not talked about in this book have never been successful in any endeavor in their lives. I am not talking about struggling, pathetic men who look at women as conquests, because they have no other conquest in their lives.

My 30-year search has led me through the night club and bar scene, hetero swinging communities, lesbian and bisexual communities, polyamorous relationships, extramarital relationships and even the BDSM (Bondage, Discipline, Sadism and Masochism) community. I have no need or desire to lie about my involvement in these activities, because it was my involvement that allowed me to gain the knowledge needed to write this book. I do nothing that I'm ashamed of and I'm ashamed of nothing that I do.

WHY DO MEN WANT MORE THAN ONE?

Abundance is the mark of success. Be it an accurate benchmark or not, abundance still stands as the indicator of wealth.

Men are expected to show their wealth by how much they accumulate. Some men have an abundance of cars, houses, businesses, clothes and money. Why wouldn't it stand to reason that many successful men would desire to also have an abundance of women? I'm not talking about men racking up a string of one-night stands, but rather, men who have an abundance of women that they consider their own.

A collection of wives has been viewed as an indicator of wealth and power for centuries. We've all heard the stories of the harems of women kept by the sheiks of Arabia. We've also heard tales about the numerous mistresses held by European royalty. And exploits of the rich American playboys are legendary. So, a collection of women is looked upon by successful men in much the same light as his exotic car collection. The women, like the cars, are loved very deeply, but not exclusively.

Even though an abundance of women can be seen as an indicator of wealth, the irony is that most men cannot achieve wealth without the desire for a particular woman or an abundance of women. Each woman plays a different role in his interaction with money.

In the case of the wife, he makes money to please and provide for her. In the case of the mistress, he makes the money to attract or keep her, and in the case of the slave, he makes the money in order to exploit, employ or control her. Regardless of how you slice it, he makes the money with women in mind.

IS IT WORTH THE RISK?

A very sincere woman asked, "With all the diseases out there in the world, why would you want to take a chance on contracting something and bringing it back to your wife?" The key word in this sentence is "want." No man in his right mind *wants* to contract any disease, let alone a sexually transmitted disease. However, what men *do* want is to sexually consummate relationships—nothing more, nothing less. The reason we take chances will never be understood, especially by someone not driven by these same desires. It's like trying to understand why a psychopath wants to hurt people that have done nothing to him. We can't understand, even though we desperately want to do so.

What scientists understand, however, is that the drive is embedded deep in the psychopath's chemistry. They also know that, by giving a chemical-altering drug to some psychopaths, they can negate the desire to act on certain violent impulses. Likewise certain drugs can be given to a man to diminish, even eliminate, the sex drive, but what woman wants a husband with absolutely no sex drive? Most women don't want their husbands to stop screwing; they just want them to stop screwing other women.

When my children reached the age for receiving the sex talk from Dad, I tried to make it as straight-forward as I could. The first thing that I told them was that "sex feels good." In fact, when done with the right person, the right way, it feels great.

I explained that this incredible feeling was the problem. Sex feels so good that some of the most devastating things a person might do in their life will be attributed to the desire for sex.

In order for a species to multiply, sex needs to be an irresistible impulse. In the wild during mating season, it becomes necessary for animals and insects to suspend all other survival mechanisms and instincts long enough to copulate. What animal is not truly at its most vulnerable state than when it is in the act of having sex?

Even though man would like to believe that his high level of intelligence should prevent him from falling prey to his own instinct, I submit that this high sexual drive may protect the human species from itself. Think about it. Man is a logical being and it's not logical to suspend the survival instinct just for pleasure. Therefore, something stronger than logic must prevail and that something is sexual desire.

It is this drive that makes a man suspend all instinct to protect his loved ones just for the pleasure of sexual satisfaction. Denial of this reality has led too many people to be unprepared when the urge strikes. Denial has led to unplanned pregnancies and the unnecessary transfer of sexually transmitted diseases.

CHAPTER 2

QUEST FOR KNOWLEDGE

In fall 2000, I met the woman who would become my present wife. I had the funny feeling that I had known her before. I had to go back some years to junior high school to finally realize where I had known her. I had a huge crush on her in 7th grade, but she had no idea I even existed. We ended up getting to know each other and I was always honest about the type of man I was, my open love for women and my desire for a polyamorous relationship.

I asked her to accompany me on the quest and she accepted the invitation. What I learned through our journeys, is that most men secretly, if not openly have the same desires, but are more practical than I in believing that a man could have a harmonious poly relationship. I also learned that many successful men lived pluralistic lifestyles, but not poly lifestyles. I found, with very successful men, that the extramarital women know the men are married but the wives didn't know of the extramarital women. Or it was revealed that sometime the wives suspected their husbands had mistresses but for various reasons said nothing.

THE HETERO-SOCIAL SCENE

My first stop in the journey was the heterosexual social scene in hopes of finding another woman who would be willing to openly share me with my wife. What I found in the traditional hetero circle was that a large number of women were willing to share me with my wife, but not openly in a situation where we all knew each other and spent time together. In fact, most of the women believed that if they wanted a decent man, then they were probably going to have to share him, but doing so openly was unthinkable.

This was my first encounter with the mistress mentality. The mistress mentality dictated that, "Yes, I will knowingly share you with another woman who is the primary woman in your life, but I want a relationship also where I mean something special to you." It was also dictated by this mentality that, "I do not wish to be part of your wife's life or social circle because within her circle I will be made to feel like a whore."

So what did most of these women with the mistress mentality have in common? I found that most had either been mistresses in the past or had worked, or at least been comfortable with, the idea of working as a call girl or exotic entertainer. Even those who had never turned a trick in their lives were not opposed to the idea of a man paying for their maintenance. They had no problem accepting money, gifts or being spoiled by a man who was the husband of another woman as long as they didn't know this other woman. Don't get me wrong. They didn't mind knowing about my wife; they just didn't want to get to know my wife.

THE BISEXUAL COMMUNITY

The next stop was the lesbian/bisexual community in hopes of finding a woman that could equally care for all parties in the relationship. This caring was not necessarily expected to manifest on a sexual basis with my wife, but rather on an emotional basis of trust and complete honesty.

My mistake in choosing this path was the assumption that bisexuality means bi-emotionality. I found that even though bisexual women could be sexually involved with people of either gender; emotionally they were as singular as their heterosexual counterparts. It was this difficulty in attaching emotionally and equally to both of us at the same time that made the lesbian/bisexual community just as barren a hunting ground as the hetero community.

POLYAMOROUS EXPRESS

"All aboard for the polyamorous express." "Polyamory" is a fairly new expression in the alternative and fetish communities. The word literally means to love many and is used to describe open committed relationships that revolved around love and equality.

I figured surely the polyamorous society would be the place to find the other woman for my world. However, it was through involvement in this circle that I found out things about my wife that I had not previously known.

What I learned is that, deep down, she really didn't want me to have another wife. What she had envisioned was our having an occasional get-together with the other woman, but not an open and committed relationship with another woman whom I saw as my second wife. This was the position she held and she had no intention of sharing it or giving it up. This attitude could never work in the polyamorous society, because their doctrine is based on equality. Neither woman would be higher than the other or over the other. Even though this is what women in the polyamorous society were searching for, it was not what my wife had in mind.

ON TO BDSM WORLD

Next stop was the town of BDSM (Bondage, Discipline, Sadism and Masochism). I stumbled across the BDSM and fetish community accidentally. Some people I ran into in the poly world also had ties to the BDSM and fetish world.

It was here that I was introduced to the concepts of (D/s) Dominant/submissive relationships and (M/s) Master/slave relationships. Polyamory in this lifestyle was often introduced as part of these M/s and D/s relationships.

It was the Master/slave relationship that drew me in, because it possibly held the secret to success for my wife and me. The Master/slave relationship is not based on equality, so the slave does not feel a need to hold a position equal to the wife.

Through this lifestyle, I met a sufficient number of women who were more than willing to come into our lives with honor and integrity and accept a position below my wife. However, my wife could not relate to these women mentally and, therefore, found it difficult to bond with them on a friendship basis.

The ideal of complete unquestioning submission to the man totally eluded my wife. Besides, the sexual practices and fetishes in this community were more than she could embrace.

THE SEARCH CONCLUDES

After five years, I concluded my unsuccessful search for an open poly relationship with my wife. This quest almost destroyed my marriage and us along with it. I could not impress upon my wife that an intelligent attractive woman with a high self esteem was not going to accept a position of second or third place. She could not impress upon me that she wasn't willing to socialize with someone with whom she had nothing in common and that she would never share the title of wife.

Unhappily, I found myself in a life much like that of most men. It was typical as far as I was concerned and I didn't want typical. I wanted poly. I mean, I had multiple women, but it wasn't poly. I had a wonderful wife who at least was willing to try; I had a bi-sexual girlfriend whom I picked up along the way that was totally respectful of my wife, and I also had a slave who had submitted to me completely and would give her life for me.

Everyone was happy, but me.

I felt I had failed, because I wanted poly and the closest I was able to get was a marriage with outside relationships kept separate but not secret. I felt that this was the only challenge in my life that I had failed to overcome.

Then one day, while discussing my problem with my best friend, I heard the words that would set everything straight. He leaned over, put his hand on my shoulder and said, "Shut the f*ck up, you stupid son of a bitch. What the hell are you complaining about? You have three women and they all know about each other. They are all happy and they all love you."

Yes, he was right and, yes, I felt like an idiot. Maybe I hadn't achieved what I had set out to do, but I truly had no valid complaint. I decided on being happy again, get focused and enjoy the rest of my life.

SHE DIDN'T KNOW HER PLACE

Things were going well until a platonic female friend of mine kept calling me at all hours. I didn't mind it, but my wife felt disrespected and couldn't understand why this friend didn't know that to call a married man so often was inappropriate. My wife came down hard, telling me, "She doesn't know her place." After all, the mistress and the slave knew better than to invade her space.

The friction was mounting when one night by sheer coincidence, I watched the DVD "Feast of All Saints." It was seeing the dynamics of the wife, mistress and slave relationships laid out in front of me that helped it all make sense.

The platonic friend that had been calling didn't know what was inappropriate, because she didn't know her place. And the reason that she didn't know her place was because she didn't have one. There is no written or unwritten protocol for female friends of married men. The boundaries are set by the friends themselves.

Even though we live in a heterosexual society, I needed to be conscious that we also live in a homo-social society. Men are expected to have male friends and women are expected to have female friends.

Because of this unwritten rule, it is difficult for a married man to have platonic female friends. If one of my buddies had called so frequently and at all hours my wife would have been annoyed but not upset. I found that she would always see my female friends as a woman first and as my friend second. As far as my wife was concerned, she had no business calling a married man so much, even if it was just a platonic relationship.

Once I came to this conclusion, I was able to ask my wife what kind of protocol for my female friends would be acceptable to her. She told me; I implemented those changes, and started to work on this manuscript the next week.

CHAPTER 3

WHY PLURAL WORKS
AND POLY DOESN'T

My first task at hand was to understand why poly doesn't work. I started this investigation with an examination of jealousy, because it's pretty safe to assume that problems of jealousy are bound to arise when there is discontentment, misunderstanding or insecurity.

Animals in the wild are rarely jealous when the male mates with more than one female. In fact it's not unusual for the bulls of any species to horde as many females as possible during mating season, yet the females don't try to stop or interfere with this multiple mating.

When necessary, nature usually provides alternative means to prevent the male from mating with more than one female. In the case of the wild canine pack only the alpha female will menstruate during mating season. The alpha male subsequently will display a protective behavior to keep the weaker males from breeding.

I realized that even though most females in the wild won't fight another female because of jealousy, they will fight to protect their place in the pecking order. Thus I concluded that jealousy wasn't the main factor in why poly relationships fail.

What I learned was that social circles are very important to women. Within these circles, there are strict protocols and pecking orders that are foreign to men.

I found that any time there is more than one woman in a room, a social circle starts to evolve. These circles form, sometimes without knowledge or desire. As most women know, it's not unusual for menstrual cycles to start and stop until all or most women in a group are in sync with the most dominant female. Women have been known to fight even kill to preserve their place within the circle.

Women in a poly household can often times fashion and adhere to their own pecking order and have love and respect for one another. Unfortunately since most families are part of larger social groups this harmony is usually disrupted. The pressure that can be exerted by these larger groups is tremendous.

A poly family can exist in peace as long as that family is not part of a monogamous-thinking social circle such as a church, social club or tight network environment. In other words, don't show up to family bowling night with two or three wives and expect open arms.

Likewise, if either one of the women in a poly family individually belongs to a monogamous thinking church or social club, she will be alienated if exposed. Alienation is inevitable unless the larger social circle also embraces the poly lifestyle as is the case in some religious orders and cults.

WHY PLURAL RELATIONSHIPS WORK

Since history had established the success of plural relationships, my next step was to figure out why and how they work. Science tells us that anything controlled by the laws of nature will always work the exact same way under the exact same conditions. One of the most basic laws of nature is; an object sitting still will remain so unless acted upon by an outside force. Simply put, if a pencil is sitting on a table it will stay there unless something or someone moves it.

Plural relationships work, because they follow basic laws of nature when done right. Below you will find the three basic laws that make up the "Pluralist Laws of Nature." For the most part they are metaphysical laws of nature but tend to be just as accurate as physical laws of nature.

1. A woman set into her position will remain in that position unless acted upon by an outside force.
2. Two women cannot occupy the same position at the same time.
3. One woman cannot occupy more than one position at a time.

Men are logical, and don't typically expect that one woman can fill more than one positions. We don't try to turn one woman into the wife, mistress and slave. Instead, we just go out and find whatever woman we need at the time.

Men accomplish this task by several different means. The most obvious is to have plural relationships where the man will have multiple women in his life at the same time. This type of relationship will split a man's time amongst several women and he'll juggle them for periods as long as 30 years.

On the opposite side of the coin is what I call a serial dater and serial husband. In this case, the man will have a series of women, each with entirely different characteristics than the last, and each fulfilling a different need at a different time in the man's life. He may also have several women in a period of 30 to 40 years, but he'll just do it one relationship at a time.

Let's look at the typical cycle of a serial husband. His first wife may be a plain Jane with a great head on her shoulders. Together, they will build their fortune. Once the fortune is built, he will desire a beautiful young woman to show all the other men how much money he has made. This stage is often called "the midlife crisis" and will precede the breakup with the first wife.

Once his sexual performance starts to slip and he becomes insecure about his gold digging second wife, he'll get rid of her while he still has some money in the bank. Finally, to take him into his twilight years, he'll marry or hire a middle-aged, less attractive woman and promise her everything he has left if she'll take care of his broken-down ass until he dies.

These two solutions, the pluralist and the serial husband, have basically gone unchanged, because even though we don't understand women, we understand what works with women. This is how our fathers did it, their fathers and their fathers before them. This can be, and often is, a difficult concept for women to grasp only because, as a general rule, women are monogamous. If a woman has need for a boyfriend, husband and handyman, she tends to try to create them out of her one man. According to the "Pluralist Laws of Nature" this will never work, at least not for very long.

WHY HE NEEDS DIFFERENT TYPES OF WOMEN

A man needs a wife for social-economic success, because we still live in a society that looks down upon a single man. This is why a swinging bachelor doesn't stand a snowball's chance in hell on being elected to public office. Women and conservatives account for a large number of votes and many voters in these groups feel there is something wrong with a man who doesn't want to get married. Marriage represents what people believe is the ability to commit, be established and be controllable. It is important to remember that the wife is a partner in planning, achieving and maintaining success.

She will be the one who reaps the benefits of his success if she is capable of maintaining her position.

Many people also perceive bachelors as the exact opposite, incapable of committing, a flight risk and uncontrollable. Men who make a conscious decision to not marry or marry and quickly divorce usually pay the price, socially, economically or both.

So why does a man need a mistress if he has a high-caliber wife to help him get ahead in life? A little-known fact is that the good ol' boy network is alive and well and having a mistress is as expected as having a nice car. We all know the saying, "The difference between a man and a boy is the price of his toys." Consider the mistress as one expensive toy. She is strictly a status symbol, one that he can be passionate about, like his cars. It is a way of bragging that, "I make so much money that I can take care of my wife in style and still have enough left over to keep a woman on the side."

Finally the successful man needs a slave to make him feel omnipotent. These slaves can hold positions such as domestic help, employees, devotees or sexual slaves. Having control or excessive influence over another's life is an indication of power. Power is what successful men strip from their slaves and give to their wives and mistresses.

Even church pastors have been known to utilize their position as leaders of their flock to gain power. There are ministers with so much control that they have told parishioners whom to marry and when. There are church leaders so influential that they have slept with half the women in their congregation and no one will say a word against them.

Nonreligious cult leaders such as Charles Manson also warrant a place in this chapter. The amount of influence that he wielded over his followers is truly scary. Ultimately it wasn't influence that Manson wanted, it was power.

IT'S GOOD TO BE THE KING

So, why does a man need this feeling of Mastery over another? More often than not, it's because most men have a deep-down desire to be king. The degree of this desire differs in every man. Some may only desire to be king of one room in the house they work so hard to provide. For others, that desire may be to hold the highest office in the land.

The original kings of this world became kings because of their ability to take what they wanted. Once power was seized by these great men they created marriage and laws so that their offspring would no longer have to fight to maintain the power garnered by their predecessors. Anyone desiring to take power at this point would be considered a criminal and punishment was swift and brutal.

Today it is possible for weak men to live like kings, because their ancestors had successfully enslaved or influenced enough people to now have organized armies to guard that power. In today's society we often label these weak men as spoiled rich kids. These spoiled brats are usually detested, because unlike their forefathers they have no respect for the people they rule over.

In contrast, strong men that are born poor know that the only way to get power is to take it and that usually means taking it from a slave, surf or peasant first and then ultimately from another powerful man. The instinct to become king still lives in us today and accounts for political dynasties and multi-billion-dollar entrepreneurs. When this instinct does not exist in a man then you more than likely will have encountered a man who is a slave at heart.

CHAPTER 4

MARRIAGE MISTRESS AND SLAVERY

Never mind what society says, marriage is a business proposition. If you don't believe it, try getting a divorce. In modern western society, most marriages start off as dating, romance and passion, but some time after matrimony enters, passion exits and a new set of priorities hit the decks. These priorities are social-economic ascent and family structuring.

Polygamy is illegal in most western cultures, because the whole idea of polygamy defeats the original purpose of civil marriage. If the original purpose of civil marriage was to combine wealth and channel it to a few, then polygamy would defeat that whole purpose. Instead of channeling wealth, it would distribute wealth. Is it possible that making polygamy illegal has always been motivated by social-economic reasons disguised as moral, ethical and religious?

THE ARRANGED MARRIAGE

In past centuries, marriages were arranged. In many civilizations around the world, marriages are still arranged. They are arranged for the purpose of creating or maintaining wealth and social status.

This seems very cruel to many western societies, particularly because our societies tend to romanticize marriage. Yet we should be careful not to believe whole heartedly that we are beyond this idea. Even though young westerners are not faced with the idea of the parents picking out their spouses, there are social environments and pressures created by parents that often lead a young man or woman to believe they have very little choice about whom they marry. For example, daughters of wealthy families are raised within a closed circle, socialized with whom the parents decide and shielded from potential undesirables. The girls will be praised for dating young men the parents like and scorned if they choose a boy who is not of their social-economic status.

Looking back on my own life, I finally understand my mother's desire to marry me off to a girl whose family she felt held the same social-economic status as we did.

Don't get me wrong; my family was not rich by any means. Both my parents came from the poor, rural South. My father became a career military man and parlayed his opportunities into an education and a good middle class life for him and his family. In the past, I thought my mother was being bourgeois, but now I'm prone to believe that she was doing her job as a wife, trying to eliminate the possibility of her heirs returning to the social-economic level that she and her husband had worked so hard to leave.

ORIGIN OF THE MAN MISTRESS RELATIONSHIP

Like marriage, the mistress relationship was born out of need. However, this need was not to attain or retain wealth, but rather a need to reward the successful man's hard work with pleasure. In a time when wives were pre-selected for a man based on class instead of chemistry, there was a good chance that the marriage would be void of passion.

Still, this was not an issue to most people, because in times when there was no middle class, people cared less about passion if they were financially successful and socially respected.

The mistress of old was usually a stunning natural beauty born of impoverished or oppressed parents. She rarely had anything to help her survive except her looks. However, she considered herself lucky, because her poor unattractive counterparts didn't fare as well. Yet being beautiful wasn't necessarily a ticket out of poverty, so to be taken as a kept woman was an honor, because wealthy men were few and far between.

A beautiful woman who was not born into the upper class but, desired to marry a wealthy man often had to settle for the next best thing, being a kept woman, a mistress. For in times when money is hard to come by, the wealthy groom's family won't care how beautiful the bride is. They'll just want to know one thing: How much money does her father have?

The young beautiful mistress was afforded luxuries that were a considerable step above that of her impoverished family, but far below the standards enjoyed by the wife of her benefactor. Some mistresses became shrewd entrepreneurs and started businesses arranging for the introduction of beautiful young women to gentlemen of means. These parlors were similar to brothels in appearance, but unlike a brothel, the end goal was to create a connection that would precede a long-term committed relationship. If the young mistress-in-waiting did not have family capable of negotiating the agreement between her and her benefactor, the parlor's Madame would step in and assist, trying to get the best possible concession for the young woman and herself.

Once the agreement was reached in placage, the new mistress was placed in a home and provided necessary servants and slaves to attend to all the domestic duties. This would fit with the benefactor's desire to keep his young beauty from becoming a run down old maid. Basically, he wanted her looking her best whenever he came around, because after all she was chosen for her beauty.

SLAVERY

Slavery will probably be the most difficult subject in this book to present, because the average westerner is appalled by the subject. Yet the average westerner still does nothing to eradicate slavery and slave labor in his own country rather than elsewhere around the world. This explains the multitude of immigrants doing back-breaking labor at wages that fall well below poverty levels, living in conditions that will rival any shack on an 18th Century cotton plantation. It is this acceptance of the slave labor economy that permits so many sexual misconducts and harassments to go unreported or unprosecuted.

There is an underground slave trade that is fast approaching drugs as the top illegally trafficked product around the world. Slaves are being brought into many modern societies from the far stretches of the world and are simultaneously being exported at an alarming rate. The economic laws of supply and demand play heavy in any illegal activity and slavery is no exception. If men and women around the world did not demand slaves, there would be no incentive to supply them. This market fuels illegal activities like human trafficking, prostitution and the abduction of young people right off the streets of our cities.

But I'm not here to write about slave labor and slavery in and of itself, but rather how this mentality plays into the psyche of powerful men who desire a pluralistic lifestyle. Even though 99.99% of the men in this world will never own a literal slave, many will use (and possibly abuse) women who have a slave's mentality or that have been put in a slave's position. These women will be used in every position from domestic service to sweatshops to corporate administration to prostitution to porn.

The position of slave may be almost as old as the wife's position. This could be, because when man first started taking women from other clans, they took them as slaves and not as wives. There were no ceremonies or celebration except for the victory celebration when she was taken from one clan and introduced into another after a battle.

There is a high probability that this didn't bother her as much as we might think by today's standards, because the conquering people usually had the best accommodations. Also, let's not make the assumption that she was getting treated all that great at the loser's domicile.

It's probable that as the conquering people rose in the ranks of their society, enslaved women gave birth to sons. Providing an heir would elevate the mother's position. After all, the mother of an heir could not be seen as a common slave. She would be given the title of wife and other conquered women would take over her duties.

CHAPTER 5

THE WOMAN'S PLACE IN AMERICA

I don't advocate that a woman's place is in the home, barefoot and pregnant. On the contrary, I believe that the woman's place is where she desires to be, whether it's in the kitchen or the boardroom, at a man's side or at his feet. It's not unusual for women to want to hold one position such as a housewife, but be pressured to occupy a different position, like bank executive.

This works in reverse, too. How many times have we heard of a young girl having dreams of being a big-time professional, but was steered towards settling down, getting married and having babies? It's common that, if a woman is a successful business mogul, she'll be made to feel like a failure if she isn't wearing a wedding band. Just as unfortunate is that, if a woman is a great full-time wife and homemaker, that she will be viewed as just a housewife. If a woman's husband is having a relationship on the side, the wife is said to be unable to keep her man satisfied. If she is the woman on the side then she is considered too inadequate to get her own man.

Sadly, the description of the perfect woman has not narrowed in the past 100 years, but rather expanded and compounded. The perfect woman now needs to be a wife, mother, mistress, executive, slut and virgin all rolled into one. The Perfect woman is now pressured by society (other women) to be a combination of Oprah Winfrey, Heidi Fleisch and Edith Bunker. In other words, she has to fulfill the roles of Wife, Mistress and Slave yet at the same time men are only expected to excel at one thing; their jobs.

THE PRICE OF POWER

I think that the American wife is the most powerful wife on the face of the earth. She has so much influence, because she has 100% of her power and 50% of her husband's.

This hasn't always been the case in America. On the contrary, less than fifty years ago, the average American wife couldn't buy a major appliance without permission from her husband.

American wives have more power than any women on the planet, but have American wives paid a price for this new-found freedom and power? Well, it is becoming common for some wives to garner wages equal to, or greater than, their husbands. And unfortunately, no matter what some say, most men can't handle their wives making more money than they do. It's not unusual for the most secure man to not marry or leave a woman that draws a bigger paycheck.

Men perpetuate a lot of bullsh*t that they would love to have a woman as successful as Oprah, but the truth is very few men could handle it. So maybe the price American wives pay is loneliness, especially if she didn't already have a man before she made it big.

THE WIFE-MISTRESS POWER EXCHANGE

Almost all relationships are based on power play. Some are a relationship of power exchange, as in any superior/subordinate relationship. Others can be more along the lines of power sharing, in which two or more people share in power of the overall group. It may also be as simple as the fact that one person makes the other person feel empowered in their life and, therefore, good about themselves.

Regardless of the dynamics, power is still a key issue. The dynamics involved in a pluralist life are no different. There is a theory that "everything we know is energy or matter." Nothing ever disappears, it just changes from one type or form to another. Since power is generated by applying energy to a particular task, it stands to reason that an exchange of power in a relationship is truly just an exchange of energy.

This theory is very important to understand, because what most wives fear more than anything is the husband taking the energy that was given to him, applying it to a task, turning that task into power and then giving that power to another woman. This fear is justified because after energy has been transferred from one person to another, the person that originally housed that energy is left empty. And this person will remain empty until she is recharged.

The basic husband/wife energy exchange starts when the husband brings the wife joy. This joy is turned into energy which the wife transfers to her husband through love, sex and romance. This energy, in turn, charges his battery so as to aid him in the success of his endeavors. After doing this, she is left empty until she is recharged by an outside source or by doing an activity that brings her great joy. The husband now takes that energy given to him by his wife, applies it to a task and reaps the fruit of his labor in the form of a paycheck (power).

Now the husband takes that paycheck (power) and gives it back to the wife in the form of property, furnishings, luxuries and financial security. The receiving of these material things brings great joy to the wife. This joy is stored in her body as energy until she, in turn, gives it back to the husband to aid him once again in being successful.

This cycle can go on for years as long as the wife and husband continue to bring each other joy. However, if the wife starts to bring the husband anguish, he will find himself going off to his daily battles with less and less energy. Believe me, wives, this lack of energy will be noticed by his superiors or clients. The less successful the husband is, the less he brings home materially. The less he brings home materially, the less joy his wife feels. And without that joy to turn into energy, she has nothing to give to him.

This cycle can also be interrupted by other factors such as; 1) The husband quits bringing home material things even though he is doing well at his endeavors; 2) The wife is not impressed by an excess of material goods or financial security; 3) Outside forces beyond his or her control interrupt the cycle, such as a layoff or lost of a contract; 4) An outside force such as a mistress enters into the picture.

Obviously, the outside interfering force that we are going to talk about here is the mistress. You see, it's possible that the mistress won't ask for anything even though she secretly desires or expects something in return for her company. Unlike most wife types, who are attracted to a man's potential, most mistress types are attracted to a man's power (paycheck). We all know that beautiful women are often attracted to successful men; however, rarely is it understood that most of these men are successful, because of the energy given to them by their wives.

For the average husband, attracting the attention of a very young, beautiful and sexy woman is a joyous occasion and joy is always transformed into extra energy. That extra energy is applied to success and the results are usually realized financially. Since it is the husband's nature to give money back to the person who brings him joy, this extra power will now be given to the mistress. The wife will still maintain her basic material possessions, but any extra money will all go to the new mistress.

The hardest part for the wife in this particular scenario is that the husband might see the wife as an empty shell of a woman, because he has taken her energy but has not refilled her. He may even seek divorce, believing that his mistress will make a better wife.

If he desires a divorce, the wife should let him go and take her half of the money, because this man is a dumb-ass and the mistress will clean him out in short time. The wife should get her half before the mistress gets a hold of it because a dumb-ass and his money are soon parted.

So, what can a wife do to help prevent this interruption to the power exchange cycle? After the honeymoon stage, keep your own battery charged. Do not rely on your husband to keep it charged. Participate in activities that bring you joy and spend time with people that bring you joy. And finally, if you are a woman that has always received joy from the attention of men, never quit taking care of yourself. Stay young, vibrant and attractive as long as you possibly can. Never allow your husband to see you as a nagging, empty vessel that is nothing without him. If you follow this advice than you'll always be a woman he fears losing as opposed to one that he dreads holding on to.

SOCIAL PRESSURE

Men basically have remained unchanged physiologically, psychologically and sociologically for thousands of years. Men have always found themselves at the top of the food chain. Unfortunately, women haven't fared as well.

Although women have remained pretty much unchanged physiologically and psychologically, social change has forced her to choose which hat to wear: wife, mistress or slave. She cannot necessarily respond to her own individual nature, but rather is forced to choose which position she desires in the man's life.

These same social pressures feed the dream of almost every little girl to become a wife, even though there are some girls who, from a very early age, know that they are not wife material. Still, they respond to the social pressures to take on the matrimonial role, hating and resenting it each and every day. Her male counterpart may be pressured into marriage; however, he is always given the social approval to sleep around if his needs are not met at home.

Society has never approved of women sleeping around, even if her husband is 100% sexually or emotionally impotent.

In the 21st Century, more and more wives and mothers are walking away from their families, throwing it all away. I believe it is because each generation of women is becoming less bound by these social pressures and, after a short period of time, realize that this is not the life for them. Social consensus declares that this woman is a bad woman. How could she not be when she walked out on her family? Is it possible that she just might have made a conscious choice not to be a wife and/or mother?

We beat up this woman, yet men have been making this same choice for millennia. Men are just now feeling the pressures to stay in a relationship to which they have committed. But let's be for real. These pressures are still not social; they're legal pressures. The pressure felt today are the strict spousal and child-support laws which encourage a man to stay. Today, if the man still chooses to walk, he at least must bear responsibility for his actions. His punishment could be as light as wage garnishment or as serious as jail time.

THE BEST POSITION TO BE IN

The inevitable question comes up: Which is it better to be, the wife, mistress or slave? There is no "best" position. Just like all positions in life, the better position is the one in which you function the best and enjoy the most. It is the one that you will be the most successful at because you have the mindset for the job. It is easy to believe that the wife will be better taken care of than the mistress but the mistress of a rich man will probably fair better than the wife of a poor man, at least financially.

Which position is considered more devoted to the man? Is it the wife who stays married for thirty years even though he has a woman on the side? Is it the mistress that stays with him knowing that she will never hold the position of wife? Or is it the slave whose sole presence is for the use and possible abuse of her mind, body and soul. All of these women can claim the title of "Most Devoted." It's just that the devotion is manifested in different ways.

Finally, if you ask which of these positions is preferred by the man, I would have to say all of them. If this were not the case, we would be living in a world of monogamous relationships and this book would never have been written. In short the man prefers that woman which satisfies his need at that particular time of his day, year or life.

CHAPTER 6

MAN'S SELF-IMAGE AND SOCIAL IMAGE

This section covers the mental make-up that has men searching for different women to interact with in their lives. Just as social groups are very important to women, social image is equally important to men. Men chose women that enhance or reinforce one or all self-images that form his combined social image. They are the social-economic image; the social-emotional image and the social-sexual image. There are many more self-images: social-intellectual, social-spiritual and social-physical. I won't cover these other self images because the reinforcement of these images comes from other men and not from women. This explains the swat on the butt on the basketball court, the cigar in the lounge after closing a big deal, combat, male bonding seminars and of course the high five in which no woman is ever allowed to participate. All of these man-to-man activities or gestures reinforce that the man has done something good, intellectually, spiritually or physically. However, there are some self-images that can be better reinforced by women and these are the ones that will be discussed further.

The economic image encompasses anything that indicates the man's ability to generate and maintain wealth. This can be anything from the type of car he drives to the size of the rock on his wife's ring finger.

The emotional image is anything that shows how the man feels about himself and others. Once again, this can be seen in the type of music or movie that might move him.

The sexual image is what tells the world how he performs sexually and with whom he performs. These indicators might be the number of women that he is dating and how satisfied they seem with him.

Control of these images is a key concern to men, because exposure of any one of them at the wrong time could make the man vulnerable to his enemies. This explains why a man will cry in the company of a woman, but not in the company of men. The last thing any man wants to do is expose his weaknesses to those that would destroy him.

A look at advertising tells just exactly how important these social images are. For example, the social-economic; the American Express Card commercial that describes how a man wanted to take his wife out for an expensive dinner and became embarrassed when his Visa card didn't go through. The social-emotional includes; the advertisement for a jewelry company that shows the man proposing in Europe to remarry his wife in front of all her family and friends. But my favorite, the social-sexual; is the Enzyte ad that shows Bob losing his swimming trunks in the pool in front of the neighbors, but he's not embarrassed because after taking Enzyte Bob now has a BIG new boost of confidence.

SUPPORTING THE SOCIAL IMAGE

The need to reinforce all of these different images encourages a man to pick a certain type of woman at a certain time in his life. Her presence tells the world what type of man he is at that particular time. Her presence and support tell the world if he is weak or strong at a particular moment. If he is able to land a high-caliber wife or mistress, this tells the world that he must be doing well economically. Likewise, if he lands a sexual dynamo, it relays to the world that he must be an incredible lover. At the same time if he loses either one of these women, he will be subject for scrutiny.

For every social image that a man has of himself, it is likely that a group will support or share this image. These groups can include, but definitely are not limited to, the workplace, country clubs, gangs, sports teams, churches, swingers groups, corporate boards, social organizations, think tanks and, of course, the boys.

For the most part, these groups are composed of like-minded people. The exceptions would be those groups where different-minded people try to achieve a mutual goal such as in the case of the corporate workplace. Even within that vast space there may be smaller subcultures of like minded people. These subcultures like most groups will share the same job description, economic status and possibly background.

Since the women that men choose are reinforcements of their social self-images, they are expected to attend social functions and shine when the man is trying to reinforce that image. All it takes is for a woman to be weak in reinforcing an image or absent from one of these group settings to create the opportunity for displacement by another. For example, if a wife doesn't want to go to his company's intramural softball games, then she will create an opening for another woman to cheer for her man when he finally hits that home run.

This seems contrary to the statement that men utilize other men in sporting events to reinforce their physical image, but it's not. In sports, the other men are teammates and opponents. The women in the stands are fans and the ones whom the players want to impress. The other men will reinforce that he overpowered or out-maneuvered an opponent, but the female fans will let him know at the end of the day if he is a stud or dud.

Unless the man is playing professional sports, there is a chance that the wife will not be overly impressed by his home run. After all, that .327 softball batting average isn't putting food on his table. But if she is not there, cheering her husband around the bases, she'll leave room for another woman to do so. And to a woman that has no man your weekend athlete might just look like an eight figure superstar.

FEEDING THE SOCIAL IMAGE

It is the wife's place to help reinforce the social-economic image of her man, by either direct or indirect means. If he chooses wisely, he will not only find someone that reflects his social-economic image, but she will also know how to work the supporting groups to her and her husband's advantage. For example, a blue collar worker who is comfortable with his social-economic status may desire his wife to dress casual, but not raggedy. This indicates that her husband is a hard-working man who takes good care of his family. Likewise, a top exec wants his wife to look like she has all the money, but not a care in the world. Even when dressed casual, she may be asked to wear heels, makeup and jewelry. When hosting a Saturday afternoon party in the back yard, the blue collar wife will probably have so much food that she'll ask guests to take some home. In lower and middle class homes, having an abundance of food is a sign of economic success. Likewise, the top exec's party may not have as much food, but the type of food, more than likely gourmet, will be indicative of success.

A man's emotional image is fueled with passion and romance. There is a misconception that men are not romantic. The reality is just that husbands are just not as romantic as boyfriends.

When a man is being fueled romantically, he carries himself differently and has a happy and positive outlook on life. He smiles at all the ladies that walk by and greets every guy with a hardy handshake and a slap on the back. Men are often far more romantic with their mistresses than they ever were with their wives. It's because most high-caliber mistresses have the same mentality or background as exotic dancers, call girls or escorts. This background means that they learned to be charming, witty, good listeners and excellent lovers. This is why they make the best mistresses. They will work hard to help rejuvenate his passion for romance when needed and his passion for life as a whole.

His sexual image can only be fed by his belief in his own sexual prowess. This is where a sexual slave can do wonders for his ego. A sexual slave can make any man feel like a stud and why not? The sexual slave will say, "Yes Sir!" to anything and seem to enjoy everything.

This may also explain why many sexual slaves have told me that what their BDSM Masters' lack in sexual prowess they more than make up for with their expertise with bondage, whips and toys. Their Master's ability to bring pleasure through whatever means reinforces that "I still got it."

Some Masters even boast of their ability to make their slave orgasm on command without touching them. I'm sure this is true in some cases, but some slaves have been known to fake it. Fake it or not the results are still the same; he feels like a stud.

Unlike the economic and emotional images, which can be seen and/or investigated easily by others, the sexual image is generally hidden. There are no credit checks or Better Business reports available to give an accurate accounting of his sexual potency. Therefore this image is usually safe as long as he has a sexy woman who doesn't tell.

EVER-EVOLVING IMAGES

Since most women believe in monogamous relationships, they believe the challenge that they face is to function superbly within each setting that encompasses the man's life. Unfortunately, all of the expectations are different for each self-image and group. What makes this even more challenging is that these self-images are constantly changing and evolving throughout the lifetime of the man.

The changing of the economic image can happen very quickly and dramatically. A sudden and well-earned promotion might be one catalyst for change; another could be the culmination of well-laid plans that suddenly result in wealth; and of course, the sudden emergence of unforeseen wealth from a lottery winning or inheritance. So, the challenge that awaits this wife might be changing from a blue collar image to an executive image. If the man was smart then he probably picked a wife that reflected where he wanted to go in life as opposed to where he has come from.

Change is not always in the "up" direction. Change can also mean the unforeseen loss of economic status due to lay off, bad investments or disaster. However, I do not recommend that the wife change the image that she reinforces unless she is specifically asked to do so. No man wants reminding of his setback and no man wants to feel that he cannot provide the things he once did. Changing might even reinforce the idea that she no longer believes that he can provide for her in such a luxurious manner. The wife may even be asked to tighten her budget and not buy anything new for a while, but more than likely she will be asked, possibly instructed, to maintain her present style and fashion.

If a woman decides that she wants the position of a wife, then she would be wise to learn to adapt and adjust to the changing social-economic status, be it from rags to riches or riches to rags. In this way, even if a fortune is lost, a first-class wife will make her husband believe that he can get it again. With her support and inspiration chances are he will.

The emotional image can change, because of how we react to something like losing a loved one or the break-up with a woman. A once-happy and confident man might find himself unhappy, even bitter, after a break-up. His confidence may be shot after losing a parent that was instrumental in his life. It is this type of change that can create a break-up between a man and his mistress, even when everything seemed as if it was going well between the two. This type of loss tends to spawn guilt feelings about not being there for the ones he loves. It can also bring on further guilt about taking for granted the ones that have stood by him through thick and thin.

More positive changes can be seen with an accomplishment such as a job promotion, school graduation and the wedding of his daughters. These types of changes are often euphoric and might bring a man to believe he can accomplish anything. This type of confidence makes a man more open to meeting and trusting others and that trust will often translate into the willingness to give to others, in this case, a mistress. Excessive giving to others is an act of passion and passion is what the man-mistress relationship is all about.

Finally, there is the sexual image. Most of a man's sexual image is created by the positive or negative reinforcement of the women with whom he has sex. The rest of this image is left up to what he projects. Generally unless a woman tells the world about her man's sexual prowess, he won't have much of a sexual image. And for most men, not having a sexual image is better than having a bad one.

Events that can positively change that image could be his sudden emergence on the scene with a beautiful sexy woman. This will definitely do it, unless everyone in the scene knows that he's suddenly come into big money. Also, a change in physical stature from exercise and/or dieting can change this image. These changes are generally seen as positive.

Unfortunately, there are other incidents that can change a man's social-sexual image and maybe not the way he wants it to change. Things like getting caught publicly with a prostitute, a man or a child will definitely change that image in a hurry. And what about the guys who are losing their school-teaching wives to teenage students, I can't even imagine the hit that their sexual image must take.

Last, but not least, is maturity. Growing older can bring on physiological changes like impotency and erectile dysfunction, not to mention the incredible shrinking cock disorder that happens to all men as we get older. So, in this case, it's just the unstoppable process of aging that could change a man's sexual image, unless he's like my grandfather who had his last child at the age of 65 with his 40-year-old wife. His sexual image changed, all right, but for the better.

CHAPTER 7

PUBLIC PERCEPTION OF
PASSION AND MARRIAGE

Even though I *now* thoroughly believe that marriage should be for building wealth, the truth is that I didn't always hold this belief. Like most people, I married for sexual passion and love my first time.

And like too many couples, when the honeymoon ended and we were faced with the task of building a future, we were out of sync. It is this lack of synchronization and communication outside the bedroom that creates so many problems in the bedroom. It is these problems that can totally strip a good marriage of love and sexual passion.

One night in a Vegas casino, I heard a young woman make the statement that, "I should have known they weren't married, because they were all over each other." Because of my lack of understanding at the time, this statement floored me. The idea that we live in a society that promotes the belief that romance and passion don't go with marriage was a very sad revelation, indeed.

Then I looked at our pop culture. Network television, especially sitcoms, reinforces an idea that the young wife's body is some type of reward for the husband's good behavior. Conversely, in more established marriages, when the woman is reaching her sexual prime, pop culture sees sex as a chore for the man who has long since left his sexual prime. When was the last time that you saw a passionate love scene between husband and wife characters? For me, personally, I can't remember.

What's sad is that this culture teaches us to marry for love, but to not expect sex after we're married. The idea of the husband-and-wife relationship as a non-romantic, non-sexual relationship is so engrained in us that it makes people no longer want to get married. It is believed that the passion and sex will disappear once the couple returns from the honeymoon. Yet the man-mistress relationship can flourish over decades without falter of the emotional and sexual exchange.

Maybe it's because, unlike a marriage, the man-mistress relationship is built strictly on passion and desire. It is not burdened with the task of building social-economic status. It is not influenced by society, because society within itself doesn't accept this type of relationship and, therefore, society only expects that it will break up. Maybe it is this feeling of "us against the world" that further fuels the passion of the two lovers. This relationship is able to grow and flourish even when impotency has been recorded in the same man's marriage.

All of our ethical, moral and religious watchdogs condemn the idea of extramarital relationships, but yet do nothing to promote the idea of passionate sex in marriage. It's almost to the point in our culture that the idea of sex between married couples for any reason other than bearing children is disgusting.

Where did we go wrong? How cool would it be if, for one week on television, the only people you got to see having wild, raw, passionate sex were married characters? Can you imagine all the single people on a show saying, "I'll be glad when I get married so I can get my freak on?"

POP CULLTURE AND PLURISM

Moral, ethical and religious social orders try hard to influence and reinforce the idea of monogamy but, they haven't a prayer in the fight against pop culture's reinforcement of sexual promiscuity. Everywhere from romance novels to daytime television, we find reinforcement of the belief in sexual and emotional pluralism.

The 1960's gave us James Bond, Hugh Hefner and free love. The '70's contributed J.R Ewing, Blake Carrington and teenage sex. The '80's gave us? Anyway, the '90's gave us Snoop Dogg, Puff Daddy and hip hop. What they all have in common is that they are success benchmarks for their particular decade. They are all known for their prowess with the ladies and their "don't give a damn who knows it" attitude. Secondly, the lifestyle they embraced showed a complete lack of reverence for matrimony and monogamy. And by the way, the '80's gave us Michael Jackson, Rick James and Pee Wee Herman. Things that make you go hmmm.

Now, in the year 2000, reality dating shows such as *Elimidate* and *5th Wheel*, present a man going out on a date with up to four different women. The climax of the show is not when he picks one woman over the others to start a monogamous relationship. Rather, the climax is when he and the women jump into a hot tub for a ménage a trois. In 2006, with everything going on in the world, the USA can't seem to get enough news about the FBI's new public enemy, Warren Jeffs, a polygamist. Meanwhile, a major cable network introduced its new controversial show *Big Love*, the story of a polygamous household. I can't wait to see what the year 2015 will come up with

PLURALISTIC NEEDS OF PUBLIC FIGURES

Mike Tyson is a perfect example of a man with many needs. His desire to satisfy all of those needs had him married, divorced, imprisoned, and broke, followed by a rebirth of his emotions, his finances and his spirit, to yet another fall. His rises and downfalls were all directly attributed to his needs.

Mike has an obvious need to dominate and he expressed the need by dominating so thoroughly in the ring for many years. However, frustrated when unable to dominate in the ring, Mike reverted to socially unacceptable behaviors like ear biting.

Mike also had a deep need to create a positive social-economic image. This creation, or reinforcement, usually comes when taking on a wife. He chose Robin Givens, who many would say had more of a mistress mentality than that of a wife.

The marriage was highly publicized, with very few believing it would work. However, in time Robin seemed to show that she had the makings for a good wife. The question then became: did Mike have the qualities of a good husband?

Nobody knows for sure, but what we do know is that a divorce soon ensued and Robin demanded a great portion of his assets. Robin cited that Mike was abusive, both in and out of the bedroom and filed for divorce.

Mike was young and single when he made most of his fortune and, therefore, Robin could not make claim that she was his muse or partner during his rise to power. Basically, she received a portion indicative of the time that they were together.

The young champion's need for sexual deviation was exposed when he was tried and convicted for sexual assault. Mike's defense was that the young beauty contestant should not have gone to the room with him, because everyone who knows him knows that he is a sexual deviant.

Mike Tyson obviously had need for more than one type of woman in his life. So it raises the question of whether Mike would still be in a possession of his millions and his wife if he had gotten a sexual slave on the side to vent his sexual deviation and frustration on. It's possible that the hurdle that Mike faced, like so many celebrities, is that he was in the public eye and anything he did with another woman outside his marriage would have come to light sooner or later and caused his life great strife.

As frustrating as it may be, a public figure or celebrity remains socially and economically joined at the hip to his wife, even if there is no sex life. A celebrity can be at the top of his game social-economically and still be in a social-sexual low.

Have you ever wondered why, even in today's age of internet porn and magazines, *Playboy* remains the benchmark of success in the adult entertainment world? The answer is simple: Hugh Hefner. Hef is a man who openly seeks out, and has, all of the different women in his life that he needs.

It has only been in recent years that Hef has become so public about his need to have different women. Even though his three girlfriends look incredibly similar on the outside-they each fulfill something entirely different in Hugh Hefner's life.

Socially, Hef made several attempts to fit into the traditional mold by getting married. This was a great gesture, but for the man who is surrounded by beautiful women, it was just that, a gesture. All of his marriages ended in divorce, surprising absolutely no one but Hef.

So now that Hef is in his 70's and has obtained all the economic status that any man could hope to achieve, he is extremely open about his poly needs. Hef is one of the few men in the world who can get away with it, because his social-sexual image and his social-economic image are one in the same.

PUBLIC OPINION OF PUBLIC AFFAIRS

When I speak of place, position or status, I'm not referring to a position or status within society as a whole, but rather a position or status within the couple's societal circle. This societal circle is determined by how many people know the couple or know of the couple. A couple's societal circle may only be the house in which they live, but it is unimaginably important that the wife be seen as queen by everyone who enters that house. Likewise for a couple with worldwide recognition and status, like the President of the United States and First Lady, it is equally important for the First Lady to appear as queen of the USA.

Let's look at two cases where the couples' societal circle was pretty much the entire world, Bill and Hillary Clinton, and Prince Charles and Princess Diana.

In both cases, it was discovered that the men had extramarital affairs. In the case of former President Bill Clinton, it was fortunate that most of the world viewed Monica Lewinsky as a simple employee, a volunteer working for the President for free. Most of the world just saw her as a young woman who was smitten by the charisma and good looks of the president. No one believed that there was a serious passionate relationship there, so we tended to view her more as a slave than a mistress. For the most part, Bill didn't lose much status or approval from those who voted for him.

It is unfortunate, however, for Prince Charles that his second wife Camilla was viewed as a vulture mistress looking for the opportunity to swoop in and devour Charles after Diana's tragic death.

The British public even speculated that Charles was involved with Camilla during the whole duration of his marriage to Di. If this is true, then this would make her a mistress and the world loathes a mistress. The acts of a mistress are considered unforgivable by society as a whole. Because the world viewed Camilla as a mistress, Prince Charles lost major approval points in the eyes of the British crown and subjects. Sorry, Charlie, you'd been better off screwing the housekeeper.

These giant societal circles, such as the Hollywood "A" list, lends to the tendency for serial dating and serial marrying. These men have needs and desires that are no different than most successful men. However, because of the public exposure created by the paparazzi, it is difficult if not impossible to have a mistress on the side. Consequently, these Hollywood hunks find themselves in one short high profile relationship after another, the exception of course being Charlie Sheen. "You Da Man."

For the average successful man, this problem is alleviated by choosing a mistress from a different circle. These circles are often segregated by social-economic walls. Special interest and hobbies are another way that these circles may be separated. For example, if the wife likes to shop, wine and dine, then the husband might choose a mistress who is a homebody without the slightest concern for fashion, dining and dancing. Choosing women in different geographical locations, ethnicities and cultures is also a preferred way to keep the circles from overlapping.

CHAPTER 8

BEST FRIEND IN WIFE

The wife's position within any man's life can be documented for thousands of years as being a place in which her primary duty is to help establish or maintain wealth and status. Within the realm of a man's success, she is arguably the most important person.

We all know that friendships forged in combat are some of the closest that have ever been documented. Since the quest for wealth is also a battle, it should be easy to see why a wife needs to be her husband's best friend.

What usually makes for best friends is the desire to share with that person. What better thing to share with your best friend than your future. Unfortunately, most men are not taught as boys to be friends with girls, so it becomes even more difficult to learn as men. The pity is that, because many men don't know how to be friends with a woman, they are prone to choose a wife for vanity reasons as opposed to a genuine desire to share with her.

Sometimes, the disadvantage of marrying your friend might be a lack of physical attraction. This usually won't bother the man as much as the woman, because his nature will remedy the situation with an outside relationship. The woman, on the other hand, is more likely to complain about such a marital problem, because she wants to find that passion in a monogamous marriage, not with outsiders.

I'm told that no woman wants a passionless marriage. Well, I haven't met a woman that wants a penniless marriage, either. Marriage is designed to build wealth. That wealth can, in turn, feed our passions, be that passion a love for the children, cars, scuba diving, fine dining, romance or even each other. However, passion without some form of wealth cannot sustain itself for long and will eventually burn out.

QUEEN OF THE HOUSE

Whether a marriage is arranged by parents or two young lovers decide to elope, whether the couple lives in a mansion or a shack, unquestionably the wife is expected to hold the position of queen. She might be chosen by parents, because she brings family money with her. She may be chosen by the husband, because she possesses the qualities and characteristic that, upon joining with him, will insure success for both. This could be a result of the fact that she understands the commitment necessary by her husband to become successful or that she is a muse who inspires her husband to success.

According to some studies of highly successful men, their wives are quite often both understanding and inspirational. In addition, the wife is often the most presentable of all women a man knows. She is the one that he can be seen with in public and be proud. She is the one that fits their social circle's idea of beauty, character and purity. It was once pointed out to me by a woman with an extremely high sex drive that, "Men don't marry sluts." The saddest thing I observed about this woman was that she was young, attractive with a doctorate degree and her own business, but a man refused to marry her because she was a nymph in the bedroom. Now she refuses to show any perspective suitors that side of herself.

WHO'S THE FAIREST OF THEM ALL

It is not unusual for a man to marry a woman based on how society defines beauty. This may explain why tabloid readers are appalled that a man might cheat on his wife with a woman that doesn't fit Hollywood's description of beauty. It is not unheard of for people to make statements like, "Why would he cheat with her when he has such a beautiful wife at home?"

The harsh reality is that she may never have been what he felt desirable, but rather what society proclaimed desirable. Since the female social protocol doesn't permit equality, comparisons are bound to arise. The wife and her social circle will need affirmation that she is prettier than the other woman. However, if it is deemed that the other woman is far prettier than the wife, they'll sympathize with the wife, because it will be concluded that the man will, sooner or later, pick the prettier of the two.

It would help immensely if men quit lying to women about what positions they hold in his life and why the women were chosen for their positions. At the same time, women would benefit by not fooling themselves as to why they are in a man's life.

Don't assume that, just because a man sleeps with you or dates you, that he necessarily finds you attractive and wants to marry you. He just might like you for other, less superficial reasons, but still not want to marry you.

A very close friend of mine has a saying that I hold very valuable in my understanding of women, "The only thing worse than a beautiful woman thinking that she's hot stuff is an ugly woman thinking that she's beautiful."

The problem that many men seem to have is that they lack the courage to tell a woman that she is not hot stuff or beautiful for fear of the woman not having or cutting off sex with him. Instead, the average man is content to let her think what she thinks. Once he's gotten his share of sex with her though he'll tire of this BS and move on.

Even the most handsome of men rarely pick women based solely on the way they look. I met a couple through a swingers' site. They were a very attractive couple and quite successful. They weren't married, though, and I soon found out why. The man secretly told me that even though his girlfriend was a beautiful exotic dancer, he hated screwing her because she wasn't real. She had fake hair, fake nails, fake eye lashes and fake boobs.

He fantasized about having sex with average-looking, but *real* women. She assumed that if he were to leave her, it would be for someone more attractive than her. She was quite surprised when he left her to marry a woman that was surprisingly plain-looking but with a high caliber wife mentality.

WHAT DOES SHE DO THAT I DON'T DO?

In the past, my wife often asked me, what kind of things I did with other women. By things, she meant what kind of relationships did we have, what kind of things did we do together, what kind of things did we do sexually and what kind of things did they do for me?

In the beginning of our relationship, I assumed she asked these questions, because of a desire for open communication and, since I have always preached that communication is the ultimate aphrodisiac, I was more than willing to tell her. What I soon found was her interest was more for the purpose of learning so she could try being all of these different women. She hoped that I wouldn't need the other women if she could do all of these things for me.

When I explained that my mistress would allow me to talk freely to her about my lifestyle without judgment, my wife would then try to listen to me without negative reaction or judgment. When I would tell her about the Master/slave relationships, she would try being 100% submissive to me. If

I told her that I would have the slave give me a manicure/pedicure and full body massages, she would voluntarily give them to me.

If I told her I could do anything sexually that I desire to these women, she would become open to trying new ideas. Even though our new type of relationship was rewarding in its own right and the sex was incredible, it lacked the status of the husband/wife relationship. She missed having the right to question my actions and to say no to me sexually. This was a right allowed only to her as wife.

My mistress was always willing to sit and listen to stories about my wife, but my wife really didn't want to hear about my mistress. Soon our talks would turn to arguments, because I would talk to her like a mistress and she reacted like a wife.

Trying to be all of these different women came at a major price, her happiness. It took away from her ability to be a great wife, because she was trying so hard to be a good wife, mistress and slave.

At that point, I came to another conclusion: one woman cannot do the job of three, at least not for very long. I realized that my wife would be willing to kill herself in her attempt to be all of these different women and more. Many businesses have had to learn that, just because a person is good at one job, doesn't mean they'll be good at all of them. The same thing holds true with the different positions that a woman can hold in a man's life. Just because a woman is a good wife, it doesn't always hold true that she will be a good mistress or slave. More than likely, it will only be a short time before she burns out and becomes discontent. And discontent women aren't loved for very long.

DON'T COMPARE, DON'T DISPAIR

The hardest part for the average wife is to not equate or compare herself to the other women in her husband's life.

I know that asking a woman not to compare is like asking the man not to sleep around. It's in the woman's nature. Unfortunately, such comparison will almost always lead to feelings of inadequacy. If the wife feels the woman is equal to or better than her, she will spend nights wondering when her husband is going to leave her. She might even initiate the separation in order to beat him to the punch. If she feels the woman is beneath her, then she'll be prone to believe that she herself is not as hot as she had previously thought or that she might lose her man to an inferior woman. And since most wives I know believe they were chosen over all other women for their beauty, this can be a hurtful blow.

Get over yourself. There is always someone prettier than you. However, if you don't know anything about this woman other than the fact that she exists, you can always keep your ego intact by just believing you are better than she is. After all, you still carry his name and that has to be some consolation. It is situations like this that the old saying, "Ignorance is bliss" becomes more and more appreciated.

The best way for a woman to not compare herself with other women is to limit what she knows about them. The basic rule of thumb is to know your husband and not his mistress. Just knowing that there is another woman or women is enough if you truly know the essence of your husband. If a wife knows and accepts her husband for who he is then there will be very little fear about what he might do with another woman.

For example, if a wife knows that her husband is a flirt, then she will expect him to flirt at every opportunity. At the same time, if she knows her husband is a dog just looking to get laid then she can also conclude that he's going to get laid every chance he can. It is this knowledge of who he as a person that keeps the curiosity down to a minimum, which is the most important thing.

VETO POWER

Frank and Judy met and, within a short period, Frank admitted to Judy that he was poly by nature and always aspired to have a poly household. Judy was impressed by his honesty and courage and chose to continue to see him. She felt that it was better to be with an honest man that wants multiple women than a liar who wants the exact same thing.

After a whirlwind courtship, they married. Frank truly felt that he had found the first piece of his poly puzzle and with her help the second deal would be a lot easier to close.

As they mapped out their plan to bring in a second woman, they found it necessary to set some basic ground rules. Judy agreed that Frank would advertise and do the pre-screen of potential wives as long as Judy retained veto power.

During the next three years, she rejected several women because she felt they weren't worthy of being his second wife.

Did I say she rejected several? What I meant is that she rejected all of them, basically all for the same reason. They weren't good enough for Frank, at least in her eyes. What Frank later discovered is that Judy subconsciously believed every woman would sooner or later turn on her and try to take Frank away from her.

The thought of losing him to an inferior woman literally unraveled her world. Secretly, Judy vowed that this was never going to happen if she had any say so and she did.

Judy wielded her veto power like a chainsaw at a massacre. The frustrated husband began to realize that his cunning wife had no intentions of ever approving a second wife and that she was just biding her time in hopes that he would one day give up his foolish dreams of having a poly family.

How wrong could she have been? In reality, it only made him more resolved to get what he wanted. Every woman that stepped up to the interview and hiring process was rejected for the same reason; they weren't good enough.

When Frank objected to Judy's vetoes, he was told that he had no discretion and that he was willing to just f*ck anything as long as it was female. Frank tried to calm Judy's fears by explaining that his desires were not just about sex, but about love.

That was the wrong answer. In fact, there is no right answer. The knowledge that her husband could possibly fall in love with another woman made things worse.

After four years, Frank finally relieved Judy of her veto power. He soon gave up on his dream of a harmonious poly household and elected to embrace the more traditional idea of having a wife and a mistress. Harmony soon prevailed, because (1) Judy knew and understood the essence of her husband and (2) she was never allowed to know too much about his mistresses. Therefore she could not compare nor despair.

Frank and Judy's problem was that the open exchange of information among them and the applicants gave Judy TMI, Too Much Information. And that information about the potential second wife always led to comparisons. Judy could only be comfortable with a woman for Frank that was exactly like her, not better, not worse and not different. And since no two people are exactly alike, no applicant was ever chosen.

Judy made a key mistake in her thinking. What she didn't understand was that any woman just like her would have the wife mentality and never would have accepted second place for long. With or without veto power, one thing became clear; Judy was never going to be harmonious with a woman that desired equal status (wife) with her.

On the flip side, if a wife doesn't know or understand the essence of her man, then she might falsely lead herself to believe that he is monogamous. This false belief will only create a problem, if the wife starts to suspect that her husband is seeing another woman, because she won't believe in her mind that he is capable of an extramarital relationship.

Investigation is usually the next step and this spy game will always lead to information about the other woman. Once again, the problem is that the more data the wife has about the other woman, the more she will compare. It's just human nature. Granted, most men are not extremely open about the kind of man they are. If this is the case, then it is impossible for the wife to know what kind of man she married. So under these circumstances, it's not her fault for being curious and pissed off when she finds out.

On the other hand some women knowingly marry a plural natured man and just live in denial. This denial is usually harmless to everyone but the wife. However; long term denial increases the chances of her snapping when the relationship can no longer be ignored.

All things considered, I would still rather deal with the wife who knows me and lives in denial than the one who knows me and tries to change me. This woman feels that if she has enough knowledge about her husband's personality traits, she can change him.

Sorry, but it's not going to happen unless he goes through a life-changing experience. Part of the process of trying to change a poly-natured man is to identify why he feels the need for more than one woman.

This being the case, the next question is bound to come up: "What do the other women provide in his life that the primary woman doesn't?" Whether the wife knows it or not, she just started the comparison process and the results will always be the same. Even when she wins, she loses. She may come to the conclusion that she is prettier, smarter, sexier, funnier and just downright better than the other woman. But then she'll again keep herself up at night with the prospect of losing her man to a woman who is uglier, dumber and duller than she is.

Bottom line: if you are fortunate enough to get to know the real essence of your husband before you get married, and if you don't like, don't agree or can't embrace the type of man that he is, then don't marry him. At the same time, if you are able to embrace his character, feel blessed, satisfied and content that you know your man better than anyone else, because it is this knowledge that gives you the distinct advantage over any other woman.

A GIFT FROM THE WIFE

If a man is involved with an outside woman and his wife knows, but doesn't say anything, he should rush out and buy her two-dozen long-stem red roses.

This is because he is truly a lucky man to have a wife that would give him the gift of a mistress. Yes, "The Gift of a Mistress." His wife may not actually deliver the mistress to him on a silver platter, but if she permits him to live in peace, without argument and disharmony, then she has truly given him the greatest gift that she can. More importantly she is maintaining her place in his life as his partner, friend and queen of the castle.

If a wife knows her man has a mistress, but desires to keep the peace, she should at least tell him that she knows and that it is her choice to leave them in peace. Let him know that this is her on-going gift to him.

If you are wondering why I say this, well, it's to disempower the mistress and re-empower the wife. In this arrangement, the wife is actually the one patting him on the head, sending him out to see his mistress. He will have nothing to complain about to his mistress and go into a protective mode when it concerns his wife, now in his eyes the most wonderful, understanding woman on the face of the earth. Once he satisfies his needs, he will race back to be with his best friend and partner.

QUEENS, SERVE YOUR KINGS

It's ironic that many women today spout the ideology that all women should be treated like queens. They assert that, upon being treated like a queen, they will make their man feel like a king. My question here is: Why wait? If treating a man like a king is quid pro quo, then you are probably not good wife material. Go ahead and apply for a mistress position and leave the wife position for the women who wish to love, honor and inspire their men to riches.

To clear up the misconception, queens never have and never will make a man feel like a king. It is the worship, reverence or fear from his subjects, servants and slaves that bring about this feeling of royalty.

A lot of wives desire to be queen of the house, but do not understand the premise that a queen is still there to serve the king, not the other way around. Stop your booing and hissing and give me a chance to explain. Women often misunderstand this last statement because of the belief that serving a man means being his maid. If a wife believes that her husband is a king, then her first and foremost duty is to serve as his most trusted advisor, not as his maid. If a queen starts to conduct herself like a servant, she can expect treatment like one.

It is also the queen's job to serve as a window for the world to see her husband's compassionate side. In this way, the husband can remain conquistador in nature but not appear arrogant or tyrannical.

A modern-day example of this spin technique was used by Brad Pitt and Angelina Jolie. I see Brad and Angelina assuming a Hollywood royalty position. Brad is definitely a king in stature, strong, handsome and top of the "A" list. He was unafraid to move past his previous marriage to Jennifer Aniston and pursue what he wanted.

Many fans, especially women, resented Brad for this decision, but a sharp Angelina quickly went about doing her job as queen and mounted a public campaign to bring awareness to world starvation. This left Brad free to continue to conquer Hollywood. If they continue in this manner, the public will quickly forget that he was even married previously and the only relationship that will stand out in their minds will be the one with Angelina.

As depicted in *Walk The Line,* Johnny Cash and June Carter employed the same spin. Johnny was a drunken rebel and had an ongoing affair with June, country music's sweetheart. June helped to rehabilitate Johnny and subsequently married him. Basically, their fans figured that if June Carter thought he was a good man, then he couldn't have been all bad.

This brings us to one of my all time favorite wives, the dear Princess Diana, may she rest in peace. Before Lady Di hit the scene, the average person around the world could not pick Prince Charles out of a one-man police lineup. However within a short time of their engagement and marriage, she had won the hearts of more people around the world and brought more recognition to the royal family than her husband could have done in a lifetime without her.

WIFELY DUTIES

Comedian Eddie Murphy once said, in a monologue that Johnny Carson's ex-wife didn't deserve half of his money in a divorce settlement, because she only had one responsibility; "to f*ck her man." This may be true when it refers to domestic duties. Let's face it, Eddie was right in his observation that she had servants to do the housework, but what about her first and foremost duty; the duty to help him acquire or maintain wealth? Is there any way of knowing if she did that job? Well, not without looking at Johnny's financial statement. But at the very least we know that Johnny didn't lose his show or his shirt that year. There was enough harmony in the house for him to maintain his work. If he had filed for bankruptcy we all would have read about it in the tabloids. So, if she brought a degree of happiness to his life that he didn't have before and if that happiness motivated or inspired him to get up every morning and go kick ass in the entertainment world, then she did her job.

Since Johnny knew beforehand that he wasn't marrying her for her cooking and cleaning, I would surmise that he married her for what she did for his body, mind and soul. If he wanted his wife to do more, then he should have married one of his maids.

The wife's position entitles her to half of everything the man makes during their time together. If the wife was there, even if only in the capacity of a muse, then she did her job. As a wife, she has helped him to acquire more wealth or maintain his present wealth. If you've ever studied a successful man who picked a horrible wife, you would probably see that he lost a lot of money during their years together.

CHAPTER 9

COST OF A MISTRESS

If the wife is considered the queen to the husband, then the mistress is like a princess. She is spoiled to a fault and cared for to the best of the man's ability. She is not expected to work if the man is able to keep her in high enough standards. He will bring her trinkets and gifts to appease her, or help her obtain a standard of living that is above the one to which she is accustomed. However, the level of luxury that he provides for his mistress will, and should always be, far below the standard of living that he provides for his wife.

A basic rule is that whatever a man spends on the maintenance of his wife and home, he should expect to spend about 10%-15% of that amount on his mistress. This might not seem like much, but everything is relative. If you take a single woman who is making $40,000 a year and add an additional $10,000, tax free, then you are looking at over a 25% raise in her income. I don't know about you, but I would take a 25% raise for just spending time with someone I enjoy.

THE POOR MAN'S MISTRESS

The stripper, although not categorized by most as a mistress, is truly one of the most lethal mistresses of all. She has but one purpose and that is to drain as much money from a man as quickly as possible. And she is prepared to do this without consenting to one sexual act.

She is armed with the ability to make men feel special. She is so good at this that even when a man is sitting next to 10 other guys, all stuffing dollars in her g-string, she will somehow make him feel special.

The most common practice of achieving this remarkable feat is the private dance. She gets her prey off by himself, away from the other men, and tells him what he wants to hear. She'll tell him how she dances for other men, but how she doesn't really enjoy it. Before the night is over, this dim-witted husband will find he believes that she is actually having an orgasm while dancing on his lap, which makes him feel like the stud of the century.

After all, how could he not be a stud when she dances on top of 25 laps a night and he is the only one to make her cum? She will make him feel just like any other mistress will make her man feel and he will reward her by giving her all of his disposable income, all $62.50.

If you're asking yourself why a man would give up his money to a woman with whom he has no chance of having sex, you're not alone. It's simply because the stripper is **his** mistress and the mistress is a reward for making "it," even if the "it" is only $62.50.

Another thing to remember is that most men don't get the pleasure of talking to a pretty young woman, never mind bumping and grinding with one. So after two weeks of hard work, his reward for making "it" is the poor man's mistress, his stripper.

Most men are not able to attract the average beauty on looks alone so they use the one bait that is universal. Going to strip clubs is like the sport of fishing. A man will go through all types of casting and waiting, hooking and netting, just so he can hold that elusive beauty in his hands for a second before he release it back into the water. Likewise, the stripper is also protected by the same type of catch and release laws. The man works all week, sweating and grunting just to hold this other type of elusive beauty in his hands, still only for a second.

Afterwards, he'll go brag to his buddies about how big the fish was or how beautiful the stripper was. Unless he has pictures, no one will ever believe him. Strippers are a short-lived reward, but nonetheless a reward. Therefore I classify her as "The poor man's mistress," because she can be afforded on just about any budget.

I AIN'T SAYING SHE'S A GOLD DIGGER

In the good old days, if there ever was such a thing, the wife had nothing to fear when it came to the mistress, because in the good old days, society would never permit the mistress to gain possession of the family jewels. In the good old days, wealth more often than not was passed down instead of earned.

However, wives today don't fair as well. Wealthy men today are often born poor and become financially successful by the time they reach age thirty. Most of these men don't think to marry in order to combine family fortunes and pass it down to future heirs. Instead, they go right to the reward stage and marry a beautiful young gold digger who will be more than happy to bypass the mistress stage and head straight for the altar.

Here's where major problems can arise. First of all, she was not chosen for what she brings to the table financially or socially; she was chosen for her looks and the passion that he feels towards her.

If the man is moderately successful, but not rich, he could easily find his retirement fund dwindling because she spends faster than he can earn. His credit can be maxed out before he can blink, because spending replaces passion. With passion gone by the wayside, he may seek out a mistress to lick his wounds once he realizes that he has married a gold-digging witch. This guy may even try to rekindle the relationships he had with the women that were by his side when he was going to college or building his wealth. You know the ones I'm talking about; good enough for friendship, but not hot enough to marry. Hopefully, she'll turn him down, remembering what a jerk he was once he got that degree or big promotion.

So, what will he do? He'll go out and get yet another mistress type, because the good wife types will want nothing to do with him. Instead of having a wife and a mistress, he now has two mistresses. Unfortunately, he's just married to one.

Unlike a wife who knows she is there because she brings value other than looks, this wife will feel quite threatened by the new mistress, because she's a mistress type herself and knows that she brings no more to the table than the new mistress. In a panic to keep the next gold digger from getting her benefactor's money, she comes up with a quick solution. She divorces the dumb bastard for infidelity and takes half of his money.

Now she is a woman of means herself and the next man will marry her for what she brings to the social-economic table; half of her ex-husband's money. What should we learn from all of this? That a successful man should fill the wife's position first with a qualified applicant then get the mistress if needed and keep her in her own place.

CHAPTER 10

HAPPY NOT BEING THE WIFE

Very rarely does the high-caliber mistress feel threatened by either the wife or the slave. More than likely, it's because she believes the average wife doesn't want her position and the slave wouldn't feel she deserves this position.

The high-caliber mistress, like the wife, may even bear children in the relationship. The man will often love these children like those from his marriage, even helping to raise them. Generally, the high-caliber mistress will be content to not petition the man for child support, if he has always contributed to the household. She will often be satisfied with this arrangement, because the children will keep her company when the man is not around. Plus the children will join them at the hips securing her a place in his life or at least his wallet.

Even though the high-caliber mistress may long for the company of her man, she rarely longs for the position of his wife. She will take it if offered, but rarely will she push for it.

The women with the mistress mentality are accustomed to their role, and many times prefer not to be the wife. They may feel that the wife's position lacks what they desire most, passion. They are often, and rightly so, under the belief that the man is coming to them, because he isn't getting it at home. 'It' doesn't necessarily refer to sex. Women in these positions know that what these men need is rarely just sex. It's about passion.

A high-caliber mistress will be happy to listen to a man complain about his passionless life, because she knows that her life is full of passion. She gets the gifts that the man used to bring home to his wife. She gets the attention that he used to lavish on his Mrs. And after she gets everything that he is prepared to give her for the day, she pats him on his head and sends him home.

On the other hand, an unscrupulous mistress with a desire to be a wife is nothing but trouble, because sooner or later, she will find a way to invade the social circle of the wife. She will be unhappy every time he leaves her to return to his wife and she will let him know. She will be unhappy every day, believing that if she were the wife she could have him to herself. She doesn't realize that, if this same man was married to her, he would still have another woman as his mistress.

LOVE HURTS

A high-caliber mistress will do everything possible to keep from falling in love. If she does, then she knows that she will dread the hour when he returns to his wife. She knows if she falls in love, she will whine when he has to leave, and sulk at home by herself on weekends and holidays.

The next time she speaks to him, she will have him feeling so guilty that he brings her a trinket, so that his visit with her won't become reminiscent of his home life. If she is hurting bad enough, she may even want to hear him lie about leaving the wife to rationalize in her own mind why she stays with him.

Unfortunately, we can't help with whom we fall in love, so the smart mistress, if in love, will work hard to stay busy with her own life, so as not to appear bitchy, needy and/or depressed. After all she may surmise that this is what he is getting at home and the last thing that he wants is two moody and bitchy women.

LYING TO A MISTRESS

For the guys that don't know, lying to a woman you keep on the side doesn't constitute having a mistress. It just means you're cheating on two women instead of one.

I know a woman that was being kept on the side by a married man. She suspected he was married, but he never admitted it. Even after she hired a private investigator to find out, he denied it. There was no doubt that he was lying to her, but since he kept her very well, she didn't push the issue at first.

She was able, with his help, to fix her credit, acquire property and improve her financial situation. The love was passionate and the sex was hotter. It was the perfect man/mistress relationship, except for one thing. He was married and wouldn't tell her. If he had only had the courage to tell her, he would still have a great mistress and wife.

She had no plans to leave him just because he had a wife. The reality is that she had more of a mistress mentality than a wife mentality. As long as he continued to do the things he was doing for her, she would have stayed with him indefinitely. Even upon confronting him with the investigator's report, he still denied her accusations. She felt she had no choice but to finally terminate the relationship.

Another type of lying that some men do to their mistress is when they are getting everything they need at home and just want more of the same at another location. He will tell a story of a lack of communication and lack of passion, only it will be a pack of lies.

This type of liar is readily identified by the general emphasis on sex in the relationship. If a man is overly preoccupied with sex, chances are he is the same way with all the women in his life. This liar will also spew out a bunch of rhetoric about staying with his wife for the sake of the children or finances. He will make promise after promise to leave his wife as soon as the problems are resolved, but the kids never grow up; the credit cards never get paid off, because this man never had any intentions of leaving his wife.

HE LIES, BUT I CAN'T LEAVE

If the mistress needs to hear lies about how he's going to leave his wife and marry her, then it's probably because her social circle is not made up of prostitutes, strippers and gold diggers. More than likely, this woman is not a mistress, but rather a wife type who just happened to fall in love with a married man. Chances are, her support group will be made up of wives and other would-be wives. This social group will listen to the rationalization for only so long before they label her a stupid bitch and cut her from the ranks. The last thing a group of married women want around their homes is a woman who will sleep with a married man.

Generally, when a woman with a wife mentality finds herself in the mistress ranks it is because she was lied to about his marriage in the beginning and now her heart is so heavily vested that she is willing to believe that he plans to leave his wife even when she knows deep down he never will.

CHAPTER 11

THE DIFFERENT BREED OF MEN

Based on so many cases and incidents of men having extramarital affairs and numerous girlfriends, we can assume that many men desire to have more than one woman in their life.

However, it's not so safe to assume that the only thing the man is looking for is sex. Different men have different needs and desires. For some men, the thrill is in the chase and knowing that they could get a particular woman if they desired. For other men the chase is not enough. It is the kill (the sex) that delivers the adrenaline to his system like a drug. And like most drugs, the thrill of the kill can be quite addictive.

Some men enjoy the attention of women, but don't necessarily want to act on it. Still other men are addicted to feeling needed and therefore they crave love and devotion. This addiction to love and devotion accounts for cult leaders who constantly push their followers to prove their undying devotion. Being commanded to give up all of their worldly possessions and their lives was the case with the Reverend Jim Jones and the "Peoples Temple" cult.

THE MONOGAMOUS MAN

This is the rarest breed of men and, therefore, makes him extremely sought-after and valued by women. This guy is singular in his love and sexual desire. If the wife ends up sharing this man, it will probably be with his children, mother, job or buddies. All of these other diversions can be as formidable an opponent as a mistress when it comes to bidding for his time, but at least the wife won't have to worry about him sleeping with any of them.

Although he may be flattered by any attention he gets from the opposite sex, he's not going to bite. A guy like this can resist the temptation of any woman. Not even his buddies can shame him into hooking up with a hot young cutie. It's just not in his nature to screw around. Guys like this are hard to come across, because they are usually snatched up by high school.

THE DOG

WARNING: If you are the wife type, mistress type or slave type you would be best advised to stay away from the dog. If you lay down with him, you will wake up with fleas, crabs and who knows what else. He openly has several different women that he cycles through like underwear. He would rather have one-night stands but will take a booty call if he has to. The thrill for this guy is truly in the kill. In this case the literal and figurative expression "kill" have one similarity and that is the fact that you can only kill something once.

The true dog doesn't want to sleep with the same woman more than once. And just as a real dog gets satisfaction from chewing on the bone of an animal that has long since been killed, so does the human dog get satisfaction from sleeping with a woman that he has long since nailed. This satisfaction however will never replace the thrill he gets from the kill. Basically he'll take an old bone but he would always rather have a fresh kill.

THE SERIAL DATER

The average man prefers serial dating, because it allows him to have a relationship of substance and, at the very least, an emotional exchange. Men have a very heavy need for emotional exchange, but for the most part don't practice this with other men. Instead, this type of man will go from one relationship to the next, enjoying the activities of dating and never entertaining the idea of marriage.

In the early 1900's, serial dating was used less frequently than today. This could be because society in the past did not favor the devout bachelor. Although a married man with a mistress was less acceptable than a devout bachelor he was better understood. People just had a hard time understanding why anyone would choose to live alone unless he was gay or a playboy—and either lifestyle was only acceptable if the man was young, good-looking and rich. For regular folks, the most preferred option was marriage and, if absolutely necessary, a mistress on the side.

It's not uncommon for a serial dater to go through a series of different types of women depending on his need at the time. Maybe when he's looking to clean up his image and become more financially responsible, he will date a wife type of woman. Once this wife type helps him accumulate a little wealth and change his image, it's on to the Mistress type.

Thanks to the wife type, he now has the tools to attract and keep her. Now it's time for fine dining, romance and fun. Yet once this new lifestyle starts to make a dent on the resources that the wife type helped him accumulate, he opts for a woman that sexually is just as hot as the mistress and just as domesticated as the wife, but not as demanding as either. He'll get a slave type.

Life with the slave type will be without a lot of drama, because she won't challenge anything he does. She'll never push for marriage and she won't demand a shopping spree, dancing and fine dining.

But it's possible that this relationship will lack something. Chances are, he will miss the wife type first, because of all the things she drew out of him, such as the way that she understood and motivated him. Unless he is financially set for the rest of his life, he will probably find another wife type to help build a nest egg. Once he finds her he'll let his slave go and possibly get married.

Unfortunately, even though he might now be married, his need to serial date will rear its ugly head. It's at this point that this type of man might make his first attempt at being a pluralist and take on a mistress. And it is at this point that he will probably fail miserably, because he never developed the temperament to love multiple women.

You see, he has been a serial dater all his life and never had to learn to love more than one woman at a time. There is a big chance that he will take the love away from his wife and give it to his new mistress. If this man doesn't put this idea of being a pluralist out of his head, he'll more than likely end up becoming not just a serial dater but a serial husband.

THE PLAYBOY

A playboy is a man who is always seen in the company of several women. He loves them and they love him but not necessarily that "I want to marry him" type of love. If the playboy is smart, he'll make sure that his entourage consists of only of mistress types and slave types. A real playboy knows that, if a wife type infiltrates the ranks and can tolerate his lifestyle long enough, he'll marry her and she will soon try to put an end to his playboy ways.

That being said, a woman is better off marrying a playboy than a serial dater. A playboy will never give the false impression that he will only love his wife. Playboys are open and honest; thus, they are great communicators.

A playboy treats all women well and the same. He'll never take love from one woman and give it to another. He'll just love them all. The final results will probably be the same as with the serial dater, but the ex-wife won't hate the playboy as much because he never gave her false hope.

THE PLURALIST

The fourth and final man is the man that generally has, and prefers, simultaneous long-term relationships. He will have two-to-three tandem relationships that may go on for 20-plus years. Each of these relationships will have very different dynamics and the roles that each woman plays in this man's life will be very different. Even though most of the relationships may start off platonic, eventually the pluralist will desire sex with all of them.

CHAPTER 12

DIFFERENT TYPES OF WOMEN

Just as there are several breeds of men, there are several types of women. The three types this book covers are the wife type, the mistress type and the slave type. The mentality of each is vastly different. Thus it is challenging for many women when they are channeled by society to hold only one specific position, "the wife." This challenge is compounded by the fact that they may truly have more of the mistress or slave mindset.

Understanding ones self leads to ultimate happiness because it is only then that the woman can fulfill the role in life that she is truly meant to play. Just as the Academy Awards are given out for leading and supporting roles in a movie, this book recognizes not only the leading ladies but also the supporting roles in a man's life.

MINDSET OF A HIGH-CALIBER WIFE

Many would say that a wife who accepts and supports her husband having a mistress and/or slave is a fool. I submit that she is not a fool, but rather a very wise woman. She is a woman that knows her limits and is secure within her position. She knows that the qualities that her husband seeks in a mistress and /or slave are not the same as a wife. She is extremely wise if she continues to work on the characteristics which make her a great wife rather than split her energies and become a mediocre wife, mistress and slave.

A high-caliber wife knows that she has influence on her man's success and failure. She won't focus on telling her husband what he is doing wrong, but rather on how he could be even better. She doesn't want to be king of the house; she wants to be queen. She takes her role as his most trusted advisor very seriously. She offers her advice as just that, advice. She does not try to force or manipulate her husband into taking her advice. A high caliber wife will be a woman, insightful and wise. She will leave being a spoiled brat to the mistresses of the world.

A high-caliber wife understands that she represents her husband and not the other way around. She is not afraid of being seen as submissive to her husband or even subordinate to her husband. She understands her place in his life and stands in it, proudly.

The high-caliber wife knows that she will see her man at his very weakest of moments, yet she will not expose his weakness to those that would do him harm or try to take that which is his. She understands that it is only because she is his wife that she will be privileged to seeing these lapses of strength. When he is weak and vulnerable, she will stand vigilant guard over him until he is strong enough to fight once again for her and himself.

If you believe these ideas are male chauvinistic, you might be right. If you believe these ideas are religious conservative, once again you might be right. If you believe they are old fashion and outdated, still once again you might be right, but a high-caliber wife is all of these things and more. She is smart, very smart and will choose wisely the man who will lead her into her future. If you are reading this book, it's only because I chose a high caliber wife.

THE MUSE WIFE

I once went to an Anthony Robbins speaking engagement. In the scheduled lineup was Donald Trump. Most of the people who came to hear Robbins speak hated Trump. It's probably because he came off as an arrogant, egotistical asshole.

One thing that was clear with Trump was his disdain for one of his former wives. He made no apologies for this intense hatred of her. He also beamed with absolute pride for the new woman on his arm. She was very beautiful, but more importantly, she inspired him. He spoke of how, when he was $9 billion in debt, all of his friends couldn't be found. Then he looked to the side of the stage and smiled at his bride to be. He eventually turned everything around to become the number-one real estate man in the New York City. It was obvious from his beaming of pride that she was his new muse.

Napoleon Hill, author of the most widely recognized book on personal achievement *Think and Grow Rich,* said that a wife could make or break a man based on her understanding or misunderstanding of the several different needs of a man. In Trump's case, it appears that one wife might have broken him and another one might have brought him back

THE PRO-MISTRESS MINDSET

If friends make the best wives, then prostitutes make the best mistresses. Once again, when I refer to "slave" and "prostitute," for the most part I mean a mindset more than an occupation or lifestyle.

In this case, I'm referring to any woman with an attitude that allows her to feel comfortable with the ideal of a married man taking financial care of her. The word "prostitute" can also mean a gainfully employed prostitute, exotic dancer or entertainer. I'm not referring to the woman that works twelve hours a night selling her body only to give all the money to a pimp. This type of woman falls under the category of a slave or having a slave mentality

One of the main characteristics of the prostitute type of mistress, whom I'll call the pro-mistress, is that she has no trouble, emotionally or ethically, sleeping with a married man. This may be the result of seeing married men fool around on the side or from her business insight that married men are her best clients.

Another characteristic she displays is her belief that her time and body have value and any man that spends time with her is going to pay for the privilege of being with her. Once again, this is because she often times has been in a trade where she has been paid for charming a man or getting down and dirty.

A pro-mistress can be very manipulative, because she knows that a married man is rarely willing to risk the exposure. In both the least and the most obvious ways, she constantly holds over him the threat of exposure. Though she wields the threat, it is unlikely that she will act upon it. Her motivation is money, so she has no desire to lose a client and start over. Don't be mistaken, though. The fact that she has no desire to start over doesn't mean that she can't do so quickly and efficiently.

Many would say that some very influential men have fallen because of extramarital relationships when the truth is that it was not the relationship, but rather, the exposure of the relationship that caused the fall. Since these icons live such public lives, any exposure would have intruded on the wife's social circle.

In the case of the exposure, where the wives publicly stood by their men, there often was only a short downfall, then a reemergence a short time later. They showed the world that they knew their place was next to their husbands and that they had a realistic expectation that their husbands would have these extramarital affairs and relations.

In fact, these same icons probably had the plural relationships going during their rise to power. And possibly part of their rise to power can be attributed to this lifestyle which makes a man believe he is a king.

For Bill Clinton and Monica Lewinsky, it appeared to the world that she was just a cog within the Clinton machine, a slave volunteer seduced into doing sexual favor for the boss. I believe, however, that she was a home wrecking mistress, a ho-mistress acting on her own desires. I believe she had a ho-mistress mentality and, therefore, lacked the ability or desire to keep her mouth shut.

She did not possess the qualities that would allow her to sleep guilt-free with a married man, much less the most powerful man in the world. A high caliber pro-mistress or slave would have kept that secret until the end of time.

It comes back to this point: If Bill had chosen his mistress as wisely as he did his wife, he probably would not have been exposed. It's obvious he chose a great wife merely by the fact that she is still with him and has grown personally since the exposure.

Once again he would have done better with a high-dollar call girl, because the prostitute doesn't want exposure, she merely wants to be paid for her time. Prostitutes know that exposure upsets their cash flow and, therefore, a high caliber pro-mistress understands the same thing. At the same time a caliber slave would have been focused solely on his pleasure and would have guarded her Master like a samurai warrior

THE PRO-MISTRESS SUPPORT GROUP

Just as the wife type has her social support group, so does the pro-mistress. This group is made up of like-minded thinkers who will encourage the pro-mistress to hang on to this man for as long as it is practical. They will actually trade recipes for cleaning a man out and protecting their own interest, just as the wives will exchange recipes for keeping women like this out of their husbands' lives.

DADDY'S GIRL MISTRESS

This suggests another type of mistress, the daddy's girl. This woman is typically younger than the man and very often brings out his paternal side.

This need may be unfulfilled for a variety of reasons, starting from the fact that he never had a daughter of his own or that his own daughters have grown up.

This void, for whatever reason, will only become painfully obvious when meeting a woman that fills it. This relationship won't be based on sexuality, but it is very possible that sex will sooner or later enter into it. This woman will be needy and possibly demanding, just as a spoiled daddy's girl might be.

The daddy's girl will be able to hold this spot for as long as she desires, because it truly is not a position that is perceived by the man as being in competition with the wife. However, if the wife gets wind of the relationship she will view this woman just as any other Jezebel competing for her man. At the same token there is little chance that the man would ever leave his wife for such a brat because she will display none of the characteristics of a high caliber wife.

THE SUBMISSIVE MISTRESS

The submissive mistress, or submistress, will be extremely self-motivated and usually self-sufficient but at the same time have a naturally submissive streak.

Her submissiveness comes from the natural desire to take care of others. Unlike the pro-mistress, she is with the married man because he unfortunately is the man with whom she fell in love and she will overlook the fact that he is married if he treats her well.

She is not intent on draining the man for all that she can, nor does she hang out with, nor respect the pro-mistress. She sees the pro-mistress as a gold digger who will get hers in the end. Not having a support group creates its own form of loneliness and isolation for the submistress, because she will not necessarily fit in the wives support group either.

The submistress would also make a great wife because of her desire to please, but she is not quite submissive enough to be a great slave. This woman will only go so far to please a man before she puts him out of her life. This submissive side of her is indeed very committed to the point of being willing to keep their relationship a total secret. She is willing to give a big part of herself and not demand that her man put a ring on her finger. The rationalization of the submistress is: "Even though I know I'm not the only woman in his life, he makes me feel like I am when we are together."

THE MODERN SERVANT/SLAVE

The slave's duties always were, and still are, to work for the family or family business. Is this really much different today? Successful and wealthy people have servants/employees working to provide a lifestyle for them that is obviously above that of the servant or employee. And, yes, getting a woman that is in the country illegally, who doesn't speak English and lives in fear of deportation to clean your house is as close to having a slave as you can get in modern-day America.

The only thing closer to actual slavery are the rich people who go to child brokers and get a young foreign girl to care for their homes and deny them education and freedom. Make no mistake, slavery is alive and well in America and around the world.

THE INTERNAL SLAVE MENTALITY

I cannot take credit for coining this phrase. The internal slave refers to a condition which occurs when a naturally submissive woman becomes so dependent on a man, that she believes she is unable to live without him. The internal slave knows her place and it is highly unlikely that she will ever contact her Master, but rather will wait for her Master to contact her. In fact, the internal slave will accept the fact that it is a privilege for her to even have that information.

The internal slave doesn't feel she has rights to this man, but rather that she is privileged to get any time at all with him. She is 100% submissive to his needs and whatever it may be that he desires she will give it to him or die trying.

The internal slave will risk alienation of everything and everybody in her life to serve the man that is the Master of her heart. She is not bound by the influence of any outside social group. If she is permitted to be part of a group, more than likely it will be a slave group. She will allow the man who she has given herself to use her body in whatever capacity he desires.

There are many men who will tell you that they can't have a woman like this in their life. Believe me, there have been occasions when every man has asked or requested something of his wife or mistress and wished that she would just do it without question.

The average man, when having a conversation about internal slaves, will picture that slave in a wife's position. Perhaps this is why he can't imagine having one. But if told he could keep his present wife and have a slave on the side for his use, then you might get an entirely different reaction.

Just about every man, has, at one time, wished he could tell his woman to shut the hell up, go to her room, wait for him and know that his orders would be followed to a T.

Some men complain that they never get sex when they want. In these cases, the man is submissive to his wife's desire, or lack thereof, and has to wait for her to ration out the sex. No man with a slave has ever had this problem.

Within certain alternative sexual lifestyles, there are relationships that are referred to as Master/slave relationships. These are outlined with their own protocols and traditions. They are designed to imitate actual slavery as close as legally possible. Drawing up contracts as well as registration of the slave with a slave registry is not uncommon in this lifestyle.

These Master/slave relationships for the most part are consensual, safe and sane, but I would be remiss if I stated that they all are. I have communicated with women that, by their own account, were raised as slaves in a slave household and even sold to another slave household. These same women, now adults, vehemently embrace the lifestyle and would not leave it for all the promises of freedom and wealth in the world.

This isn't surprising if you look at the history of slavery in America. Many slaves, when given the opportunity to separate from their masters, did not. These types of decisions may be attributable to what is widely recognized now as the "Stockholm Syndrome." The ability to separate from a capture is more difficult than one might imagine.

An internal slave rarely fears competition from the wife or mistress. It is the loss of her position and opportunity to serve that she fears losing. Even though this internal slave knows she doesn't have the right to tell her Master not to accumulate other slaves, she will let her feelings be known by how she treats a new slave that enters the workplace or house. Even slaves need to know that their alpha slave status is not up for grabs. The established slave will accept the new slave only after taking her through a form of breaking or training. If the new slave can handle everything dished out to her, then she'll be welcomed, but she must know her place as little sister.

ACTUAL SLAVERY

There is an underground that imports and exports people throughout the world as slaves. Asian women are brought to the Americas under false pretense and American women are sent to Asia under equally false pretenses.

This practice is one of the lowest acts that man is capable of committing, but it happens every day. A San Francisco newspaper published a four-part story on a young Korean woman who, in order pay off $60,000 in credit card debt, accepted a job offer to work as an entertainer/hostess in the United States. She was given the impression that it was a totally legitimate deal. She was flown into Mexico then smuggled into the U.S. where she was forced to work as a prostitute in a massage parlor until she was able to make her escape.

SLAVERY THROUGH ABUSE

Another type of slavery that exists but is not labeled slavery is at the hands of an abusive spouse or father figure. This condition can also occur in women that have been broken through abuse by a male figure. After the breaking she will find herself with such low self-esteem that she will attach to the first dominant force that gives her attention. Listen to some of the stories of these abused women and you will no doubt understand that they were enslaved. It's not unusual for women with this slave mentality to have an inappropriate idea of what a man should be. She may find herself believing that a man is any member of the male species that has the physical strength to make her submit.

SLAVE OF HARD KNOCKS

Kristin was a street hardened ex prostitute with more than 8 years under her skirt. By the time she met Claude she had more than 30 misdemeanors and 7 felony arrests. After she left her pimp she enslaved herself to another man who she called husband. She slaved in everyway to please him domestically and financially. It was for him that she received her last conviction and a four year sentence for laundering money. She was caught transporting a quarter of a million dollars for her husband's brother. This last arrest retired Kristin from the street life. Illegal hustling was basically the only life she had known since age 16 when she was turned out by her pimp. But eight years on the streets and four in prison were not the worst of it. Kristin had endured nine irreversible years of violent rapes by her brother. These vicious rapes went on from the time she was five years old and did great damage both physically and psychologically. And like all people the events that take place in our formative years shape what we are to become in the future.

Claude and Kristin had met through the swinger's lifestyle. Sexually they clicked almost immediately. She informed Claude that she needed her sex rough and raw in order to get off, a result of the nine years of sexual abuse. Claude having been exposed to a wide variety of sexual practice was more than willing. She reiterated to him that even though she was submissive in bed that was where it was to stop. Kristen was at a point where she was trying to turn her life around and the last thing she needed was to give up that type of control again. Claude was agreeable with the terms and hoped from the start that it would turn into at least a great friendship. They seemed to hit it off and Kristen slowly revealed her past history. Claude was never put off by what he heard. In fact he seemed to embrace her more as she shared her painful experiences. Kristin had found herself at this point in her life racking up a string of one night stands whenever Claude was unavailable. She was using sex with no attachment as a way of staying in charge of her life. Unfortunately she found it to be very lonely most of the time.

Yes, Kristen was in charge of every relationship she had but one; her boss. Even though her boss wasn't exploiting her sexually he was working her like the slave that she was. He even violated labor laws but Kristin was so afraid of losing her job that she refused to report him. In the past when Kristin had worked the streets she was known to work herself to death for her pimp. She did this to please her pimp and now she was taking this same outstanding work ethic and trying to satisfy her boss. She received a small promotion, enough to keep her around. However deep down she knew that she would never go any higher because of her arrest record. She thought this just might be as good as it gets.

Despite all of Kristin's efforts it became very apparent to Claude that she was truly a slave at heart and had gone from serving a pimp, to a husband to a boss. One weekend it also became apparent that she would never serve him. He called Kristen one night after not having talked with her for a couple of days. She worked swing shift so he invited her out for a drink after she got off work. Kristen was agitated, stating that she had been in the hospital with bronchitis since he had last seen her. To make matters worse she had to work nine and ten hour days all week without a day off. This was because her boss had refused to hire someone to cover for her. She cried that she even had to work nine hours the day she went into the emergency room. She complained that she had needed him during this trying period and that she was hurt because he had taken a break from her.

Claude had no guilty feelings about taking time away from her. She had shown signs of getting sick prior to his absence and actually told him that she thought it might be bronchitis. He asked her if she would quit smoking and drinking until she got better and she refused. Now he could hear her coughing on the phone and it was apparent that she was still fighting the illness. She told him that she had planned on going home to rest but that she would join him for the drink if he wanted. He informed her that he didn't want to encourage her to drink until she got better and that she should just go home and rest. When asked if she was still smoking she replied that she had no intention on stopping. She also informed him that if he wasn't going to honor his invitation to her for a drink that she would just go home.

Frustrated, Claude went to the store, picked up some juice and a get well card. He went by her house dropped them off. As he looked at her sitting up in bed pathetically coughing and smoking he decided that their relationship would be a lost cause. He knew that he couldn't be involved with someone displaying such obvious self destructive behavior. He refused to be with someone who would kill herself for an abusive pimp, a shiftless husband, even her boss, but not heal herself for him. But the harshest reality of all was that Claude had to accept that he wasn't domineering or abusive enough to command her and this hurt more than anything.

Kristin found herself in a Catch 22. Women like her are open game for overly dominant and abusive men. Although they don't want to respond to these types of men, this is what their bodies are accustomed to doing.

She didn't have a man in her corner to keep the predators from swooping in and devouring her, because she didn't respond to protective men, only abusive men. And although she wanted a man in her life for support, she was unwilling to voluntarily submit to him. Any man that wanted her submission would have to take it.

All she had ever known was forced submission and this thinking would forever have her serving and sacrificing herself for the benefit of strong handed or abusive men. In a nutshell Kristin was destined to remain a slave, be it a street slave, house slave or corporate slave. Her master would inevitably be the one strong enough or mean enough to use or abuse her.

THE EMPLOYEE SLAVE

Threatening loss of wages is coercion and the tool of choice of many supervisors, managers and employers. This might not constitute literal slavery, but if the fear is great enough, it constitutes psychological enslavement. Single women with children are the prey of choice for these types of predators and it needs understanding that what they hunt is not sex, but power. These men consume power by stripping it from female employees and feeding on it.

The employee's indebtedness and obedience is their aphrodisiac. It becomes common-place amongst certain men to sexually release this power on the same employees who they drained to get it. They will do anything from verbal harassment to sexual molestation. If the sexual advance is unwanted, it's called harassment and, thanks only to the laws which govern labor relationships, the woman can sometimes exact any form of justice.

THE SWEATSHOP SLAVE

Sweatshops are a type of slavery that big business perpetuates every day in the name of free enterprise. For the most part, thanks to modern labor laws, these sweatshops are kept to a minimum, but the laws have been unable to eradicate them. Many men, when given reign over these predominantly female work crews, have escalated incidences of sexual harassment against them but they never get reported. The reason being is that these sweatshops are predominantly staffed by poor, uneducated, single mothers, illegal immigrants and possibly abused women. More often than not they are put on a per piece rate of pay, worked for 12 plus hours a day, seven days a week and are lucky to scratch out minimum wage. The men that run these shops feed their egos with the feeling of power over these women. They walk in with the plan of growing rich off the sweat of these women and have no fear of retaliation or incarceration.

THE CORPORATE SLAVE

The corporate slave may live a life of solitude without any man in her life but her boss. Therefore, she looks forward to returning to work each day and serving the only Master she knows in hopes of getting even the slightest amount of praise. But she won't receive it because many a supervisor or manger knowingly steps on these women to advance their careers. They assume all credit for the ideals and hard work of their charges, and will take offense and holler, "Reverse discrimination" if a woman is promoted over them. It is unfortunate that when a few of these women are promoted that they tend to continue the cycle of abusive and demeaning behavior that was perpetrated on them. It's not unexpected though when you think about it. How often do we hear of children who continue the cycle of abuse by their parents?

The corporate slave is often educated and extremely capable; however she more than likely will have an innate fear of men, especially men in charge. Her low self esteem may come from being ostracized in school, prior abusive relationships or even an abusive father.

I can't help but think about the character Jane Hathaway from the television series *The Beverly Hillbillies*. She slaved for her boss without appreciation. Her life revolved around the office and her boss, Mr. Drysdale, who would do something incredibly demeaning to her whenever he needed a power boost. But for all of the abuse she endured she stayed with him forever because she was truly enslaved to him and the company. Her only source of pride was one; that she was great at her job and two; she was the top slave in the secretarial pool.

VOLUNTARY SLAVE

Even if slavery didn't exist, the Master/slave relationship would. It's simply human nature. Some women will always find pleasure in caring for others. Some women will always take pride in pleasing the men that control their lives. Some women will even be willing to endure his pain after a hard day at the office. They will stay with the man of their choice after being beaten and broken. There is no want or desire that she will not try to fulfill and she will live to hear him say, "Well done!"

No wife or mistress can ever threaten her spot. Only the presence of another slave can unnerve this ever-diligent servant.

There is a woman who, for no apparent psychological reason, desire with every fiber in her being to serve the man in her life. She knows this deep down in her heart and wants to serve and give to the point of being willing to lay down her life for her man. That is the mindset of the voluntary slaves. She possesses the same career military attitude that drives a soldier to serve and would even give her life for the honor.

The voluntary slave more than likely grew up in a household watching women break their neck to make sure the men in their lives were happy. The women that they saw might have been married to the men but their attitudes and actions were more indicative of a slave than a wife. The voluntary slave might endure verbal and even physical abuse but she recognizes this as discipline and punishment. She will only question the treatment if it goes above and beyond what she considers good taste or if it incapacitates her keeping her from fulfilling her duties.

At this point, it is appropriate to mention that I unequivocally do not condone true slavery. I do not condone keeping a person against their will. However, I also do not condone taking a woman's choice to serve a man away from her, simply because it is deemed psychologically unsound behavior.

The reality is that many women consciously chose this lifestyle, because it is in line with how they see themselves. These women do not look to serve just anyone, but rather desire to choose the man to whom they will give themselves completely. Their level of devotion and servitude goes far beyond the level that most women desire to give. I'm enclosing a poem from a woman that I only name as "slave with honor." It is printed here with her permission.

TO SERVE OUT LOUD

I AM NOW RECEPTIVE TO THE IDEA THAT . . . IT IS TIME FOR ME TO STOP WHISPERING AND TO START SERVING OUT LOUD. STOP HIDING! STOP HOLDING MYSELF BACK AND PLAYING MYSELF DOWN (I AM A SLAVE)! STOP WORRYING ABOUT HOW I LOOK AND WHAT PEOPLE ARE SAYING (I AM A SLAVE). STOP LISTENING TO WHAT PEOPLE ARE SAYING AND TRYING TO FIND OUT IF THEY ARE WHISPERING ABOUT ME (I AM SLAVE) STOP WAITING FOR SOMEONE TO TELL ME THAT I AM OKAY OR TO MAKE ME FEEL SPECIAL (I AM A SLAVE) SERVITTUDE IS SPECIAL! IT IS A SPECIAL GIFT. THIS IS MY LIFE! NOW I'LL TAKE MY GIFT AND LIVE IT OUT IN THE OPEN! I'M DECIDING TODAY THAT I AM GOING TO SERVE OUT LOUD! SERVING OUT LOUD MEANS HAVING THE COURAGE TO BE EXACTLY WHO I AM WITHOUT APOLOGY. IT MEANS ADMITTING MY MISTAKES WITHOUT BEATING MYSELF UP. IT MEANS NOT TAKING WHO I AM AND WHAT I HAVE FOR GRANTED. RELEASE ALL SHAME! RELEASE ALL GUILT! I CANNOT SERVE OUT LOUD IF I AM HIDING BEHIND WHO I WAS BEFORE REVELATION. SERVING OUT LOUD MEANS FOCUSING ON WHO I AM RIGHT NOW AND THAT'S A SLAVEGIRL! TO SERVE OUT LOUD MEANS SHOWING UP AS MY AUTHENTIC SELF, WITHOUT MY MAKEUP OR MY WEAVES. IT MEANS ACKNOWLEDGING MY SHORTCOMINGS AND CELEBRATING MY STRENGTHS. SERVING OUT LOUD MEANS BROADCASTING MY NEED TO SERVE, MY LIKES AND MY LIMITS AS THEY ARE RELATED TO MY FEARS AND FRUSTRATIONS. IT MEANS THAT I MUST LET PEOPLE KNOW EXATLY WHO I AM AND EXPECT THEM TO BE AS THRILLED AS I AM ABOUT BEING A SLAVEGIRL! IN ORDER TO SERVE OUT LOUD I MUST HAVE FAITH IN MYSELF AND IN MY MASTER. I MUST HAVE COMMANDS I AM TO LIVE BY AND STANDARDS BY WHICH MASTER CAN GOVERN AND GAUGE ME. MOST IMPORTANT, IN ORDER TO SERVE OUT LOUD I MUST LOVE MY MASTER ENOUGH TO SERVE AND OBEY HIM WITHOUT CAUSE AND\OR JUSTIFICATION. WHEN I DO THAT I CAN SERVE OUT LOUD AND BE VERY PROUD ABOUT WHAT MY MASTER WOULD TELL THE WORLD ABOUT ME. UNTIL TODAY, I MAY HAVE BEEN SERVING IN A WHISPER. JUST FOR TODAY, I'M TAKING ONE STEP TOWARDS PUMPING UP THE VOLUME. I'M STANDING UP IN MY SERVITUDE! I'M STANDING UP

AND BEING A SLAVEGIRL! TODAY I AM DEVOTED TO BROADCASTING THE
TRUTH ABOUT MY SERVITUDE!

THE SEXUALLY DEVIANT SLAVE

Finally, there are the women that have heard romanticized stories of
bondage and sado-masochistic seduction. These are women with rape and
kidnap fantasies. Some may possibly be serial killer groupies. Such women
would probably lose it if they ever had to experience the real rape of a stranger
or a narrow escape from a sadistic serial killer.

This woman is a sexual deviant and sexual slave only because her sexual
practices deviate from "normal" sexual practices. She believes she is a worthless
piece of meat and dreams of being used as a total slut slave, caged or chained,
waiting for the next time the Master needs her.

The sexually deviant slave is the pimp's dream, because he knows that
she'll do whatever is asked of her—and do it with pride. She will work all
night, walking the streets and freely give up the money to him, because her
satisfaction comes from being used sexually. The sexual deviate slave will
prefer use over love and pain over hugs.

Punishment is a big turn-on for most sexually deviant slaves and they often
rationalize their love of pain as a well-deserved discipline for bad behavior.
She will take that attention in the form of punishment, call it love and believe
that, if her master didn't discipline her, then he must not love her.

It is not unusual for this type of slave to have a masochistic streak in her,
but it is not always necessary. She will accept her punishment, be it physical
or mental, and take pride in her ability to learn from it.

To recap: With the exception of the voluntary and the deviant slaves, these
modern day slaves feel disempowered and unable to say no. On the other
hand, the voluntary and deviant slaves feel completely empowered, because
they are psychologically free to submit to the men of their choosing.

CHAPTER 13

FILLING THE POSITIONS

It is imperative that a man knows himself. Men need to know what they like and what they don't like, what they want and don't want.

In choosing a wife, choose a woman that desires to be in your social circle, not just tolerates your friends. Honesty is the key, but honesty must first manifest within yourself before you can be honest with others.

The best time to confess any idiosyncrasies is usually within the first few hours of meeting a woman. Don't wait, because it will only get harder to tell her. You may believe that your lifestyle, preferences or skeletons might run her away. I'm not saying to try and freak her out, but confess them honestly, without shame and you stand a better chance of finding someone that will share those quirks. Only through this honesty will you have any real chance of finding the right woman to share your life with you as a wife, mistress or slave.

It is hard to fathom why men lie to women about being married. I can honestly say that I have never run off a woman by telling her I was married. I have, however, run off plenty by telling them I was happily married.

Regardless of whether a woman has a wife, mistress or slave mentality, she may not necessarily hold the institution of marriage as sacred. However, there seems to exist an unwritten code amongst women that says, "Hands off!" the *happily* married guy. I guess women feel at least one woman out there should have a good marriage. Let it be known that if a man brags about how great his marriage is and how much he loves his wife, he will find that he just might have talked himself into a purely platonic relationship. This new friend will be so faithful to his wife that he won't be able to get her in bed with a gun. It is only when I have told women of my poly nature and that I have an open relationship with my wife that they have stuck around and considered having a relationship with me.

CHOOSING AND BEING CHOSEN

This is the 21st Century, America, and men need to understand that women are also sifting through potential suitors for their life's partner. Unlike men, women have always been smart enough to choose a husband for social-economic reasons. Unfortunately, now that the sexual revolution has come and gone, women are finding themselves making the same mistakes; they marry for looks, sex and passion, just as men do.

There are tens of millions of women in this country and men need to learn to stay honest and keep moving until they find the woman with whom to build a future. Thanks to the internet, there is no excuse for a man not to shop around and be honest.

A man can meet thousands of women near him or half-way around the world, if he so desires. However, he should guard against letting the Internet becoming his social circle.

BELIEVE THERE IS SOMEONE OUT THERE

Once the man has gotten to know himself and learned to tell the women he meets the truth, it is time for the next step.

He must learn to believe that there is someone out there who wants to share his lifestyle and passions. Sometimes, even friends with the best of intentions will unwittingly discourage a man by saying that he'll never find someone who enjoys whatever he enjoys. Exploring alternative lifestyles has taught me that if you like something then there is definitely someone else out there that likes it just as much.

Having the same interest is nice, but having a love or passion for the same things is the key to success. And it is not important what that interest is. The common interest may be sports, religion, hobbies or even shared sexual activities such as swinging or BDSM.

What's important is that the man put it out there from the very beginning. It is this type of honesty that will allow him to sift through all of the women that can not share fully in his life.

RIGHT PERSON FOR THE RIGHT JOB

My mother has a saying, "You can't make a purse out of a pig's ear." To this day, I've yet to see anything to prove her wrong. In this case maybe it should read, "You can't make a wife out of a Mistress."

Men who know they are bound for a pluralistic relationship should refrain from trying to make a wife out of every woman they love. The fact that he falls in love with her doesn't necessarily make her wife material for him. It's always possible that he may have fallen in love with her, because she is great mistress material.

I know a woman who, during a short period of her life, became a submissive mistress. During this period, she also befriended the man's internal slave. After a period of time in this relationship, she decided to break up with the man.

She spoke with the slave and both women had agreed that he was a jackass, but when the time came to make the break, the slave couldn't go through with it. The mistress tried for over a year to help the slave make the break, but she was unsuccessful in severing the connection.

The mistress had a difficult time understanding why the slave couldn't break from the man. The answer lay in the understanding that the mental makeup of the slave and the mistress was so very different. Although there was great passion in the mistress relationship, the man could never get total control over her. The reason is that she had other men in her life that she could use for support when his demands became unreasonable.

The slave, on the other hand, was totally dependent on the man, both emotionally and psychologically. She had no other men in her life and felt that she owed her existence to him. To make things more difficult, the slave had accepted a job working for the man, thereby compounding the dependency.

This story illustrates the distinctive differences in the positions that women hold in a man's life. More importantly it shows the difference in the mindset of the women that hold these positions.

BE A MAN, TELL THE TRUTH

Men who desire pluralism shouldn't be afraid to say that a particular woman would not make them a good wife. He is really doing her a favor, because it's highly unlikely that he will make her a good husband. He should be honest and tell her that it's not that she won't make anyone else a good wife, just not him.

At the same time, if a woman is genuinely wife material, the man needs to understand that she is not going to hang around indefinitely without him finally putting a ring on her finger. Sooner than later, she is going to demand her position as his wife. And it is advisable for the women that are good wife material to not give more than two years without receiving a wedding proposal.

If it takes longer, then he truly is not interested in marrying you. Move on and find someone who is ready to marry—and not because he's been given an ultimatum. It is a woman's right to demand the position of wife when she is a wife at heart. This type of woman isn't moved by social pressure, but rather by the psychological and physiological cues that her body sends her.

If a man continues to couple with a wife type, without the intent of marriage, he should plan on the average relationship lasting no more than four years. Right around year three in the relationship, the would-be wife will start to receive social pressure from her social support group, a/k/a "the girlfriends."

"The girlfriends" will more than likely be married or at least in hot pursuit of a husband. Would-be wives tend to hang out with married women simply because they have a like mindset. "The girlfriends" may start to introduce their single friend to their husbands' eligible bachelor friends.

This is a smart move, because the husband's friend might have the same mindset of the husband and be open to the idea of marriage. In fact, the bachelor friend might even be looking for a wife himself.

However, just because a man is husband material don't assume that he is monogamous husband material. At the same time, don't assume that, just because a man is a bachelor that he lives a pluralist life style. He may be so mono in his nature that he doesn't want to share his space with anyone, not even the woman he loves.

If a man loses the woman he loves because he isn't willing to marry, he shouldn't get upset. This moving on in her life is expected, because deep down in her heart, she always felt like a wife. Deep down, she won't be happy until she fulfills her destiny and, deep down, the man needs to admit that he can never truly makes this type of woman happy.

WHAT DO YOU WANT?

Bernie wasn't looking for a wife when he met Michelle. Fact is he wasn't looking for anything at all. You see Bernie was a devout bachelor and had plenty of female company whenever he wanted. Now, a lot of men claim bachelorhood but the truth is that a lot of them are just single men. The difference is that a bachelor is single because he doesn't want to get married, and the single man is single because he can't get anyone to marry him.

The two met at a local lounge, the kind of place where everybody knows your name. Well, everyone knew Bernie but Michelle was a stranger to the group. She was brought in by her best friend who although married still had a slightly wild streak in her. She was always trying to get Michelle to go out but Michelle was a homebody with her primary focus on raising her teenage daughter. She had been abandoned by her ex-husband and left without much but her pride and tenacity. With those two qualities, however, Michelle built her life and career. She combined those qualities to create a life for herself in which she could purchase anything and everything she needed. Nice homes, furnishings and cars were no longer beyond her reach. Although Michelle was pitied by some of her married friends because she was single, she was also envied by them. You see, the women she knew were married to very successful men but were not as personally successful as their husbands. Michelle on the other hand was as successful as their husbands and didn't have to deal with a man when she didn't want to.

Michelle was a good looking woman with a beautiful smile, shy but very personable. She was also raised strict Catholic and was way behind Bernie when it came to sexual experience. Bernie was a handsome world traveler and former military man. He kept himself in good shape, spoke different languages and could be extremely charming. Some considered him a smooth operator but really he was just a man who enjoyed the company of women. He had also been married once before and never really quite recovered financially from the divorce and heavy child support payments. However he was humble and counted his blessing for he did have his freedom and a positive attitude.

After introducing the two, Michelle's friend left them to talk. They talked as Michelle nervously tore at a cocktail napkin in her hand. Bernie came out very honest and admitted that he loved women and planned never to get married unless he could find a woman that could embrace his lifestyle. Michelle seemed okay with that. They exchanged numbers later and hugged goodnight.

Bernie and Michelle grew close, extremely close. Their relationship lacked nothing. There was love, passion, respect and commitment to be there for one another. In fact, with Michelle's help Bernie even found himself climbing out of debt and accumulating a little wealth. Michelle on the other hand was learning how to have fun in and out of the bedroom. The fact that Bernie wasn't willing to commit to a monogamous relationship didn't create a problem because Bernie hadn't met a woman that could hold a candle to Michelle nor had he met someone that seemed a better match for him.

That was until he met Lynn. When meeting Lynn the connection was obvious. She was attractive, fun and also a world traveler, someone who he could swap stories with. What really set the hook in Bernie's mouth was that after a short time she revealed that she was the type of woman that could be with a man like Bernie and never ask him to give up his bachelor ways. In fact she traveled so much that she said it would be perfect as long as she got attention when she returned home. She actually encouraged him to see whomever he wanted. Even though Bernie had grown to love Michelle very deeply over the years he found that he had also fallen in love with Lynn.

Bernie had no desire to breakup with Michelle or Lynn. He just wanted to have both of the women he loved in his life. Michelle would complain about the situation and Bernie would fire back, "Well, what do you want?" She would cry, "I want you, but I don't want you to be with other women." "You're not telling me want you want" he would challenge; "you're telling me who you want." Michelle stood her ground and pronounced "I don't want a man who has other women." Bernie came back again, "Stop telling me what you don't want. Tell me what you want." Finally in a fit of anger and frustration Michelle shouted at the top of her lungs "I want a monogamous relationship." Bernie confessed that he could never promise her a monogamous relationship. They sadly parted and went their separate ways.

A week later Michelle met another man through the same group of women that she had met Bernie. He spied her through the group and went right after her. He introduced himself and to her surprise his name was also Bernie. Though disturbed by the coincidence Michelle was elated by the attention. This Bernie was tall, handsome and financially successful. But more than anything when asked by Michelle what he wanted in a relationship he answered "I want a committed, monogamous relationship. I want a wife." About a year later they were married and I truly believe they are headed for Happily Ever After.

You see there is a big difference between knowing *who* you want and *what* you want. It's only when we can express what we want without guilt or hesitation that we have a chance of getting it.

SHOPPING FOR A MISTRESS

The man should find a mistress that is in no way associated with his life or the life of his wife. The mistress should travel in an entirely different circle and work in a different industry. She should have no contact with his social life, not even the bar where he hangs out with his buddies or the field where he plays intramural softball.

The minute that he is seen with her in any social setting that his wife may cross, he will have started a chain reaction that will, sooner or later, get back to her.

It is at this point that the wife has every reason in the world to be jealous, hurt or spiteful. It is because her man unwittingly, but perhaps knowingly, brought another woman into the wife's position. It is the position of the wife to be seen in her social circle with the man not the mistress.

FILLING THE MISTRESS POSITION

All in all, I would say that the mistress is the hardest position to fill. The good mistress has some of the traits of a good wife and some of the traits of a good slave, but she is required to use them differently.

When a man spends time with his mistress, he is not looking to spend it with an idiot. He wants someone who is a good listener.

This humble and attentive woman will listen as you complain about your day at home or work. She will not take sides, but tell you the truth. She knows that you need to hear that. She will even allow you to complain about your wife and never suggest that you leave her. Instead, she will kiss you on the forehead and pat you on your butt as she sends you back to her to make things right.

Don't expect however that you'll be able to complain endlessly about your wife and she'll sit up and listen to it forever. The prize mistress will dump you, because she will have realized how weak you are and lose total respect for you. If this happens, you have only yourself to blame.

Truth be told, most women in the mistress spot would rather hear the man brag about his wife than complain. At least with bragging, there is the reassurance that she is in good company and that if this man with this wonderful wife chooses to spend time with her than she must be special too.

The mistress hunter should be looking for sexual passion, but at the same time, he should be looking for someone who has no desire to be a wife.

Her reasoning can be various, from understanding her own needs, to having no respect for married men, to possibly being married herself. For whatever reason the good mistress is content to stay a mistress as long as her needs are being somewhat met.

A prize mistress accepts, and expects, that she will never be taken care of as well as the wife. Whereas, a ho-mistress, will find herself scheming on how to supplant the wife and take her position within this man's life.

MARRY A MISTRESS AND SHE'S STILL A MISTRESS

If a man does decide to take his mistress on as a wife, he should refrain from changing the style of the relationship. It needs to be understood that this relationship was not formed for the same reasons that most marriages are and, therefore, should be governed by the same rules as their man/mistress relationship. If he allows her to claim a space in his life that the wife vacated, he will surely be sorry unless she is willing and able to lose the mistress mentality. There is a big difference between taking on a mistress as a wife and shopping for the next ex. If a man is truly just shopping for a wife, he should look for the top of the line wife as opposed to the top of the line mistress.

In some instances, the transition from mistress to wife is successful, but it doesn't happen overnight. It takes both partners' conscious effort to foster this change. The husband has to constantly remind her that her role is no longer to spend wealth, but rather, to help build wealth. She, on the other hand, has to learn to deal with the fact that she would now be the one left at home while her husband goes out and spends time with his new mistress. I've always speculated that, if a man marries his mistress and suddenly becomes faithful, he really wasn't committed to making the first marriage work. If he had been as faithful to the first wife, he might still be with her.

DUMB DOG

This section is dedicated to my father, who always said that a smart dog never sh*ts in his own bed. I've already discussed the idea that a man should never shop for a mistress in his workplace. This section will deal with the man who isn't actually looking, but just accidentally falls into an office affair. It's not unusual for the man that employs or manages a female workforce to identify with a particularly great worker. Now, even though she is employed in a slave/servant role, she more often than not has the makeup of a great wife and will become his most trusted advisor at work. It is very common to have a bond with this type of woman, because she is self-motivated, intelligent and loyal to a fault. This bond can even start to feel sexual and the man may be tempted to make her his mistress.

Don't do it, don't do it, don't do it!

She will fall in love and so will he. This is bound to create major problems, because she will basically become his second wife. She will hold the equivalent position to the home-wife, except it will be at work.

Stop for a minute and take into consideration that many successful people spend more time at work than home. This is a formula for devastation if the home-wife is not as good at what she does as this new job-wife.

The job-wife will shine every day you see her, only to further accent any shortcomings that the home-wife has. If the home-wife finds her husband suddenly eager to go to work when he dreaded it in the past, it will be painfully obvious what's going on. Out of loneliness or desperation, the home-wife might make the offer to come to work at the job. The husband will refuse for obvious reasons, even if she is more qualified than the job-wife.

What we now have is a power exchange. The husband is stripping power from the home-wife and giving it to the job-wife. This is the same woman who previously was in a slave/servant position. If the husband allows the power exchange to go any further, it will only be a matter of time before a breakup and a changing of the positions. The job-wife never had a mistress mentality so she more than likely will want the home-wife's position. This is because she was a single woman with a wife mentality working in a slave's position.

If the man divorces his wife and offers her the position, she will take it. Simply put, the single woman with the wife mentality is always looking to get married, sometimes even if it's to another woman's husband.

ANOTHER STUPID DOG

The other stupid dog might ask: what if the man falls in love with an employee that has a mistress mind set. Accordingly, she won't want to take the wife's position. Well I agree that there are plenty of women in the workplace with a mistress mentality. In most circumstances, they would probably make for a great mistress, but in the case of the workplace, it is a serious taboo. Sexual harassment cases are rarely brought by women with slave mentalities or wife mentalities, but rather by women with the mistress thought process, because the mistress will be more likely to flirt with, and accept the advances of, the boss. She will do this with her mind focusing from the beginning on what she can get out of it. She may be satisfied with special treatment, or she may not stop until she has settled a high-dollar lawsuit paid by the company and/or the boss.

The best advice is to avoid the social circles that will possibly overlap with your wife's and just stay clear of the workplace all together.

CHAPTER 14

A HAPPY HUSBAND DOESN'T WANT ANOTHER WIFE

Most women know when their man is with another woman. So then it should also be noted that when a man is satisfied with his wife, he will **not** chose a woman of the same characteristics.

Allow me to reassure the wife that her position as wife is rarely in jeopardy if she is good at being a wife. However, if she is a wife with a slave mentality or a mistress mentality, her position is always at risk. This is because neither the slave nor the mistress mentalities focus on the accumulation or maintenance of wealth and social status. Unless the man is retired or independently wealthy, there is a good chance that he is trying to achieve these objectives. He will instinctively know that he has a better chance of retiring independently with a wife as opposed to a slave or mistress type. This being so he'll always be on the lookout for a high caliber wife type.

One thing I disliked about the movie *Waiting to Exhale* is that Angela Bassett's character was a consummate wife type and as a couple, she and her husband built a fortune. It seemed highly unlikely that he would leave her for his secretary (slave) for no apparent reason. I'm sorry, I just don't buy it. What makes more sense is that he was stupid enough to have an affair with the secretary and his wife found out, thus throwing him to the curb like a bag of garbage. Now that makes more sense to me.

NON-COMPETE CLAUSE

If a man chooses wisely, he can eliminate most of the competition between the wife, mistress and slave, but if he inadvertently chooses women of the same makeup, then he's bound to find himself in deep trouble.

This is the mistake a lot of men make when they reach the decision to take on an extra-martial relationship. Men should not choose a mistress that could be his wife. If he does, then expect that when he discusses his marital problems with her that she will feel that she can replace his wife. She might even encourage a breakup, believing that he is ready for a changing of the guards.

PROTECTING THE WIFE'S POSITION

The husband's first priority should be to tell any perspective mistress or slaves that he is protective of his wife's position and has no intention of replacing her. This protection should not be reserved for just the position of the wife but also joint assets as the following story implies.

WHAT'S IN A TELEPHONE BILL?

Conrad, a married man, found himself involved with a Daddy's girl mistress type who was needy beyond means, at least beyond his means. You see he met this woman with no intentions of starting anything. These types of meetings can sometimes be the most dangerous because there are no preset limits. Why would he need a preset limit if he had no intention of starting a relationship?

Things progressed quickly and before he knew it they were talking day and night. The talk was passionate, lustful and raw. It was open without judgment. Although he hadn't realized it at the time it was just what his body was craving. It seemed that they had covered light-years worth of time in less than a week. Before he knew it he was cashing in some frequent flyer miles and on a plane to see her. It was spontaneous and caught her totally off guard. As she drove into the passenger pickup area at the airport he could see her search the curbside for him, smiling like a little girl whose father had come to pick her up from school. It seemed like the car barely stopped when she popped out and ran to him. She called out "Daddy" and they hugged each other tightly.

As he sat in the passenger seat on their ride back to her part of town he could see the little girl in her, as she smiled non-stop. He hadn't seen a look like that since his own daughters were but small children. That look that makes every father feel as if he is the greatest man on the face of the earth, that feeling that only a baby girl can make him feel.

They stopped at her favorite local restaurant and had a bite to eat. She sat across from him beaming with pride ready to introduce him to anyone that would ask. As they sat and talked across the table it became obvious that the noise from the surrounding tables would keep them from having a private and intimate talk over dinner so he got up and moved to her side of the booth. She was excited yet scared. She rationalized to herself that it was okay to be with him, to want him even though she had just met him online a week earlier. However there was no confusing the attraction and electricity that jumped back and forth from body to body. They wanted each other and yet there was no rationalization for each of them taking the chances that they were.

He put her at ease when he reached into his back pocket and pulled out his wallet. He handed her two forms of ID and insisted that she make a safe call to a friend. She felt better, safer that he had taken into consideration how fast this was moving and how easily they could have broken all reasonable protocol for safe dating and meeting. He explained that he had come only in hopes of meeting her and spending even a few minutes with her would have been enough. He had no expectations only hopes that if he were to meet her that the attraction would be as strong in person as it had been over the phones which they had spent countless hours talking.

Even though every thread of common sense told them not to go back to her place, every thread of passion and lust told them differently. There was never a feeling of being uncomfortable. It wasn't long before they found themselves at her apartment. The typical chatting ensued but they both knew what was in the back of their minds. They retired to the bedroom both of them tired and having to get up early so he could get back to the airport for a 6:00 a.m. flight out. Since he had no intentions of staying the night, he booked as early a flight as possible so he could just sleep in the airport if needed. As she came out the bathroom dressed in a T-shirt and panties he began to wonder who was seducing whom. One of the things he found most desirable about her was her extreme comfort with herself and her sexuality. In very few words she made it clear that she was his for the taking if he so desired, and he did. Their bodies were aflame and everything that night was deep, raw and hard, the kissing, the love making, the sex, everything.

As his plane slowly pulled away from the ground the next morning it struck him what had just happened. It struck him how totally consuming this relationship could be if he let it get out of hand. He had always made a personal vow to himself that he would never let an extramarital relationship impact his marriage, but this one could if he didn't get a handle on it quick.

The weeks went by quickly as Conrad worked to make time to talk to her everyday even if only for a minute. The feelings were real, not just sexual, and they would literally talk for hours when time permitted. And talk they did freely and unchecked, that was until he received his cell phone bill. He had gone over his preset minutes. Devastated, he called her and broke off the relationship.

Maybe some of you are thinking what an asshole this guy must be to just break it off like that. Try understanding that because he didn't set limits in the beginning it was necessary to set them later. He needed a gauge to measure his self-control in the relationship or lack thereof.

The phone bill became that gauge. As a married man, he already had an agreement with his wife about the phone plan. That may not seem like much to some, but it was a plan that they agreed on as husband and wife. It was a plan that they felt gave him enough time and flexibility to talk to whomever he needed as much as he needed. It was also a plan that they mutually agreed would not overtax their means.

The overage indicated that he was starting to act beyond his means. It indicated that he was being consumed by his desires. It wasn't about whether or not they had enough money to cover the bill, it was about the husband's responsibility to protect the wife from his extramarital relationships and that protection extends to the protection of assets also.

PROTECTING THE MISTRESS' POSITION

If the mistress finds out that her man is sleeping with yet another woman besides her and his wife, she will become at least as jealous as the wife. A lot of people find this ludicrous, because the husband is cheating on his wife with her. The mistress doesn't mind sharing the man, but she doesn't want to share the position.

Once again, the emphasis should be on the man to create a secure spot for the mistress, especially if she is a good one. Most good mistresses won't come onboard if they feel the man is just a dog and she is just one in a long line of conquests. If the mistress is just another number, she should recognize it and move on.

A man, hopefully, will take himself off the market once he has filled all slots. If he went through the selection process with any diligence, this shouldn't be a problem. If he started the search with his penis instead of his head he'll probably screw this up too.

PROTECTING THE INTERNAL SLAVE'S POSITION

Generally, the only woman in this rectangle that understands her place, whether she desires it or not, is the slave. This may be attributed to the slave having such a low self-esteem that she doesn't feel worthy of being more. The other side of the coin is that she has such a high understanding of herself that she doesn't desires any other position than the one she holds. This is the woman that gives so much and asks for so little in return.

Even though all she desires is to please, she will also need guidance and reassurance in feeling secure within her relationship. Unlike the wife and the mistress, she will worry less about being replaced and more about being released. The woman with this mentality is often the most fragile one of the bunch and may even need protection from both the wife and the mistress, if they become aware of her existence.

CHAPTER 15

DO OUTSIDE RELATIONSHIPS
LEAD TO DIVORCE?

Any woman that is still reading might be thinking that I promote extramarital relationships. Regardless of whether I do or don't, they continue to happen in increasing numbers. Modern wives not accepting outside relationships the way their foremothers did have been a large factor in the rise of the divorce rate.

This is not to blame women for our rise in divorce, but maybe the reason that the rate was lower before was because of the woman's willingness to cope with plural relationships. A woman who married by arrangement or necessity rarely had a belief that she would be the only woman in a man's life. In modern times, when women marry out of love, they are more prone to believe that love is their guarantee of a monogamous relationship, and it's not.

AN OPEN OR CLOSED RELATIONSHIP?

Open marriages are becoming popular again. The '60's brought us free love, the '70's brought us swinging and the '80's brought us HIV. The '90's gave us a renewed attempt at monogamy and abstinence. It was during the '90's that people looked at promiscuous sex as Russian roulette with an HIV bullet. However, researchers in the '90's were steadfast in their search for a cure, or at least drugs that will keep one from dying from the disease.

In the '00's some have changed their view of HIV from seeing it as a death sentence to living with a life-long injury. Another thing is that we live in an age of extremist and high-risk takers. It's a natural progression that unprotected sex is back on the rise, not just in men but in women, too.

The question now becomes: Do you, as a wife, desire a relationship where you know who, what, when and where, or do you prefer the bliss of ignorance? Each has its advantages and disadvantages. The advantages of open communication include that it helps forge a stronger bond and a far more heightened sexual arousal towards the one with whom you are communicating.

Most people in totally open or swinger relationships have a very high sexual interaction with each other, even after 10 to 20 years of marriage. That doesn't mean that a couple in a marriage that's having problems should go out and start swinging. On the contrary, if a marriage is having problems, try counseling that is designed to get you communicating, because chances are this is where the real problem lies.

On the other hand, if you are communicating very well and the communication has revealed that the problem is boredom and redundancy, than swinging might be an option to consider.

The disadvantage is that not everyone can truly handle open communication. Some women desire the communication of an open relationship, but insist on being able to react as if they were in a traditional monogamous relationship.

All this does is create a situation that results in massive arguments. These women would want to know all the details, and then all hell will break loose after hearing it. To put it in the words of a cinematic Marine officer, they can't handle the truth.

In a closed relationship, there is no communication about outside relationships. The advantage of the closed relationship is that both people have found one less thing to argue about in a world where there is always plenty to argue about. Between raising the children, financial problems and just dealing with the everyday problems of scratching a living, it seems the last thing that a marriage needs is arguments over another woman. Couples in closed relationships can maintain an amicable coexistence for decades and it has been proven by a long history of marriages in which the man had extramarital affairs from the start.

One such family legacy is the Kennedy's. It has even been said that one Kennedy brother advised a younger, apprehensive brother on his wedding day that he was not expected to be monogamous, just married.

The disadvantage of a closed relationship is that it inevitably sets up the mistress as the confidant to the husband and not the wife. Looking at the Kennedy situation, a mistress became so comfortable with the idea of being the inside woman that she actually showed up at the President's birthday party and sang a sexy, and now legendary rendition of *Happy Birthday*.

This last scenario can be avoided, if the couple makes a conscious decision to agree that there may be outsides relationships during the course of the marriage, but also agree to not talk about them. In this case, a couple has created the advantage and the opportunity for open communication before the extramarital relationships even start. The couple can set guidelines, priorities and protocol that when followed can help to keep peace, harmony and respect in the marriage.

The couple can also agree to revisit the guidelines at any time that one spouse or the other feels there is a problem. This type of communication keeps the wife from ever being perceived as the outsider in the man's life. It also negates the probability that the husband will find anything negative to say about his wife in the presence of another woman. His wife will after all be the most understanding woman he knows.

CHAPTER 16

COMUNICATION HELPS, A LOT

Why does the mistress know more about the wife than the wife knows about the mistress? It's because the high-caliber mistress will never tell the man to quit seeing the wife. In other words, a man can tell his mistress anything and she'll never give him grief over what he has just said. That's what puts the mistress in a far more emotionally secure position than the wife, even though social-economically the wife's position is far more secure than the mistress' could ever hope to be. It is this same social-economic security that keeps many people in a relationship long after the love is gone.

What a shame that it is more difficult for the wife to communicate with her husband than for the mistress. If she could, then she would be the one that knows everything about her husband instead of the mistress. She would be able to make it through any unforeseen public exposure and maybe guide her husband in choosing the right mistress who wouldn't expose any of them

DOES MARRIAGE ENCOURAGE LYING?

For the most part, married people lie to each other. The lies are usually small ones, about little things around the house like taking out the garbage. But if either partner finds themselves in a sticky situation, look out, you might hear a politician-sized lie.

What really needs examining is the motivation of the lie. Any lie that I have told in a relationship or marriage was strictly because I didn't want to be judged and condemned, when prior attempts to tell the truth in these relationships indicated this would be the case.

The rebuttal: "Well, you shouldn't be doing anything you are not supposed to do." The problem with this response is who are we to tell each other what we should or shouldn't be doing?

We live in a world full of rules and regulations and many of us are raised being told what to do and what not to do. Unfortunately life isn't this simple. Just as locks are made for honest people, rules are made for the conformist and any married man with a woman on the side is not a conformist.

Mandating rules give people a false sense of security that, when breached, leads to incredible feelings of betrayal. For example, most people get married and assume that there will be monogamy. This assumption is only believed because the rules of marriage state that husbands and wives are supposed to be monogamous. However, if man is capable of breaking the rules of God and society with respect to the most heinous crime of murder, why is it so inconceivable that he'll break the laws of God and society with respect to the minor infraction of infidelity?

Most people are taught to follow the rules as opposed to being taught to take responsibility for their actions. People that thoroughly believe in the idea of taking responsibility for their actions rarely feel a sense of betrayal when someone they love breaks the rules. Sooner or later we all break the rules.

Dictating to each other in a marriage what we can and cannot do can be very risky, especially if the desire is to keep communication open and honest. What a lot of people don't realize is that open and honest communication should be the ultimate goal, not conformity. Conformity and control will never work on an extended basis unless one person has the strength to enforce that control.

Communication, on the other hand, has a proven history of bringing about peace and good will. It is good will that makes people desire to maintain self-control in society and it is good will in a marriage that makes a partner want to maintain self-control.

Unfortunately, open communication cannot be achieved where there is judgment and condemnation. Judgment, condemnation and punishment usually lead to a breakdown in communication and that breakdown will inevitably lead to a breakdown in intimacy.

Some food for thought: Is it possible that people who sneak around with each other get so sexually aroused because it takes such great communication to do it well? I mean the planning, the coordination, the synchronized lying and picture perfect execution requires the same communication as a covert spy operation.

I'VE GOT SOMETHING TO TELL YOU

It had been a year since Shane started surfing the internet. At first it was just for tidbits of info but he soon discovered the darker side of the internet, online porn. It wasn't long before he was spending one to two hours a night online. He was becoming more and more exposed to alternative sexual behavior and lifestyles and with that exposure came a new acceptance to things that he had been closed to in the past. He was becoming more and more open minded and wanted to try something new.

That night when Shane went to bed he curled up next to his wife of 10 year, Shirley. You see Shirley had noticed the change in Shane's behavior but never said anything about it. She wasn't really into computers and so she knew very little about the internet and had no idea what Shane could possibly be doing in his home office all night. What she knew was that her husband was home, not out running around with the boys or trolling the bars for some other woman. What she didn't know is that Shane had been trolling online on a couple of the dating sites. These sites weren't the ones that tried to match up two people for a long term relationship but rather these sites were for swinging, and affairs were not uncommon. He wanted so much to try some of the new things that he had learned about with Shirley but he just knew she wouldn't be up for it. Besides he had known her for over 10 years and she never even mentioned wanting to try some of the things he was now discovering.

It wasn't long before Shane started chatting with an online fantasy woman. She was also married and feeling lonely, ready to branch out and try something new. They had exchanged pictures and were planning their first rendezvous. This was exciting to Shane. He now popped out of bed in the morning instead of dragging himself out. He became more conscious of his appearance and hygiene. The first date was set for Friday after work. Shane had planned on telling Shirley that he was going to have to work late and that he would pick up something to eat in the city.

Friday morning came and Shane was excited about the upcoming date. However when he looked at his wife that morning he got a funny feeling in the pit of his stomach. He dropped his eyes, kissed her on the cheek goodbye and raced out the door. That afternoon Shane called Shirley from work and informed her that he planned to work late. Without question or whining she simply stated "Okay honey, I'll see you when you get home." Before Shane could even check his words he spoke "I love you sweetheart, bye." He smiled then quickly dialed up his internet date and finalized the plans for their date but something seemed different

He didn't seem quite as excited as he had been. He shrugged it off to first date nerves and went back to work.

As Shirley opened her bag of tacos that she picked up on the way home she thought, "What a treat." It wasn't often she got to eat Mexican food because it gave Shane heartburn. She had just finished her first one when the front door opened. It was Shane. "I thought you were working late tonight" she stated. You see it was Shane's regular time to get home. Shane looked at her and replied "I've got something to tell you." He told her all about his last year of online surfing and even of the date that he was to have. He told her of all the different perverted things that he had read about and seen online and how he was ashamed to talk about it with her. Shirley gently stroked his face and in a voice as sweet as honey replied. "Thank you for talking to me first. Would you like to try some of those things with me?" Shane's heart raced as a monstrous smile came over his face. He took her hand and put it on his now rock hard member and said "I haven't had wood like this since we first met." Shirley giggled "Mmmm I know, I know."

Communication will always create and maintain passion. Entertainer Will Smith once said, "Jada and I work on our marriage every day, because we are different people today than we were yesterday." The two understand the importance of communication, even if it's something that they think the other may not like hearing.

If your man tries to talk to you about his desires before he acts on them, let him. Don't judge or chastise him, because chances are if you do, he won't ever tell you again. And the day that he stops wanting to tell you things will be the day that he starts telling someone else. Just try to remember that lying can be stifling to a marriage, but truthful communication can be stiffening.

MIDLIFE PASSION

The previous story of Shane and Shirley is a perfect way to introduce this next passage. The need for reinforcement of the social-sexual image often reemerges in men during the time we often refer to as "the midlife crisis." I prefer to call it "the midlife passion."

It is during this midlife passion that the man may decide to take on his first mistress. As I stated earlier, a mistress knows how to make a man feel desirable and a man leaving his sexual prime feels anything but desirable.

These can be the best of time or the worst of times for a married couple. Just as the man is experiencing a need to feel desirable, more than likely so is his wife. She may have taken the backseat to his job or business for 15-plus years and now she is ready to share romantic passion with her husband.

Even though these two may know each other socially, economically and psychologically, very rarely do they still know each other sexually. It is this lack of knowledge sexually that keeps them from sharing their newfound need for sexual passion.

It's necessary to understand that passion is often generated outside the bedroom, but consummated inside. That is why mating rituals exist in nearly all animals. Dating, courting and nightclub pickups are the human form of mating rituals.

Most couples put these rituals away once they leave the dating phase and enter into their matrimonial phase. However, during the midlife passion, we just might see a regression to the bars and nightclubs, maybe even a church, in search of an extramarital affair.

Just think about the advertising slogan for Las Vegas: "What happens in Vegas stays in Vegas." The slogan is an invitation to come to Vegas to party, meet someone, take them to your room, sleep with them and then go back to your boring life in Smalltown, USA.

Plain and simple, the slogan is about extramarital affairs. In a strange place, among strangers, we can be a totally different person and, therefore, interact sexually without fear of exposure and damage to our social-economic circle.

In layman's terms, it's not enough to just sleep with someone else. Hell, you can do that in your home town and never be caught. The social-sexual image needs feeding and as such people want to flirt, dance, touch, drink and socialize before sleeping with someone else. And they want to be able to do this without it getting around town and destroying everything they have worked for.

It is during this sexual rebirth that couples might investigate and participate in swing clubs and alternative lifestyle play parties. After one, two or three decades together, people still have a need to feel sexually desirable. And this need can rarely be satisfied by a long-term mate. For some reason, a husband or wife of 20 years telling you that you're so sexy doesn't seem as convincing as a total stranger telling you. Swing parties and swingers' clubs are often a good way of reliving those dating days for midlife couples. They are a nice alternative to the dance club scene. There's just something uncomfortable about going to a club where the average patron is half your age and the music and dances are un-relatable.

Sharing a public display of sexuality such as flirting, seduction and possibly sex with the wife can often diminish the man's desire to take on an outside relationship. The man, at this point, is able to openly express this need to feel desirable by other women and his wife can be right there. However, this solution will not work unless the man is equally at ease with sharing his wife with other men. It is also why, within most swingers groups, strict rules against dating someone else's spouse are implemented. The idea is to share sexual desires, not to encourage an ongoing relationship with someone else's partner.

The midlife passion stage can be the worst of times or the best of times. However if a couple doesn't find a way to bring the passion back it is probable that one or both will seek an outside relationship.

CHAPTER 17

YOU MADE THIS MAN
NOW SLEEP WITH HIM

Sexual attraction more often than not is a reflection of how one person makes another person feel about himself. If a woman makes a man feel stupid or weak then don't expect him to believe that he is a raging bull when it comes to sex. At the same time if a man makes a woman feel prudish and frigid, don't expect her to come like Niagara Falls at his touch.

A lot of women take great pride in their ability to manipulate the men in their lives, however few realize that the price that they often pay for this control is the lost of passion and dedication from the very men that they control. Every man knows when he is being manipulated and that manipulation only serves to make him feel disempowered. He sometimes feels he can't help it because of the undying devotion he has for the woman. More often than not a woman's manipulation and control causes great self resentment and feelings of emasculation which might lead to impotency.

When wives get together and congratulate each other on their ability to get what they want through manipulation, they often don't understand that they are helping to create not only an opening for a mistress but the motivation for their husbands to seek one.

A woman in her early 50's once confided in me about her sexual relationship with her husband. I knew that this woman was controlling and demeaning. She informed me that she believed her husband to be impotent. I responded with: "Are you sure he's impotent or is it that he just doesn't want to f*ck *you*?"

This wasn't the response she wanted and she quickly dismissed the conversation. I responded that way, because I was able to recall my own situation when going through problems in my first marriage. My wife awoke at 2:00 a.m. to catch me masturbating. When asked what I was doing I snapped, "I'm cheating on you!"

This caught both of us off-guard. I felt my ex-wife was manipulative and just the thought of touching her made my penis go flaccid. When communication and openness are replaced by manipulation and control, there is a high chance that passion will be smothered along with love.

Final note; this previous statement assumes that the man doesn't have an attraction or strong sexual desire for dominant, controlling and manipulative women.

YOU GOT HIM, NOW WHAT?

The only thing more important than knowing how to get the man of your dreams is knowing when you've got him. It is in a woman's nature to need the daily reassurance that she belongs to this man and that he belongs to her. Unfortunately, it is not in a man's nature to voice this on a daily basis, so it is sometimes very difficult for her to know. This is not a knock on women; it's just a difference in our need and ability to communicate.

This lack of feedback and it's affect on the woman can best be illustrated by a technique that my brother showed me in martial arts training. He instructed me to grab him by the wrist as tight as I could. Normally, when a person is grabbed around the wrist, the first reaction is to pull back. It is this reaction that lets the aggressor know whether or not he has a firm hold. However, my brother did something totally unexpected. He did nothing. He relaxed so much that I was unable to tell if I really had a good grip. It was this lack of feedback that made it almost impossible to tell if I had him. I found myself readjusting my grip every fraction of a second trying to get a response from him.

Similarly, it is the readjustment that becomes very annoying to a man that has relaxed into the relationship. It's a constant signal that the woman is unsure of her place and it will sooner or later be interpreted as nagging, bitching or neediness. So the only other thing she can do is to wait for him to pull away. Then she can receive some feedback as to how tight of a grip she has on him. Her ability to keep him from getting away is what gives her assurance that she genuinely has him.

I WOULD DIE FOR YOU

Many women expect their man to be willing to lay down his life for them because most women in a serious relationship would do so. The problem with this train of thought is that most men do not expect nor want the woman to lay down her life for them.

What men want is for women to share with them in three basic parts of their life: the economical, emotional and the sexual. Men don't want women to dominate and control these settings; they just want women to share them.

WE KNOW DRAMA

Some women say that they are not looking for drama in their lives, but the reality is that humans, like all creatures, live and grow from struggle. Drama is struggle and without struggle there is no life.

It is that struggle that lets us know that we are alive. Therefore, life without drama is usually no life at all. When a woman has a man who doesn't struggle, she finds life with him boring.

If a woman truly wants a relationship without drama, then she should find a man without children, wives, ex-wives, "baby's mamas," hobbies, a job, friends or a life. Maybe instead of telling everyone that she wants a relationship without the drama and finding herself bored or alone, she should try saying that she wants a relationship worth the drama.

USING HIS INSTINCTS TO KEEP HIM INTERESTED

Sometimes a man needs to know that his woman is not just desirable to him, but to other men as well. I'm not saying that he wants to see his woman with another man, but he doesn't want to believe he's the only one who's attractive to her, be it mentally, physically, emotionally or sexually.

When a man thinks about losing his wife, he is usually thinking along the lines of losing his partner. This loss conjures up visions of settlements and equitable splits of family and assets. Yet when this same man envisions the loss of a mistress, he knows it's a loss of good sex, love and passion. Finally, when he thinks of losing his slave/servant/employee he thinks about how hard it is to find good help.

Staying desirable is the greatest challenge for the woman. This is usually because she tries to change and become desirable in a position that she doesn't hold. For example, if the wife tries to become more physically and sexually desirable to compete with the mistress, it is possible that her husband may not even notice the differences. This is mostly because he may not see her in that vein. However, if the wife goes back to school or gets a promotion, he'll definitely notice and be very proud. These types of achievements also place the woman in the eyes of other successful men that appreciate her as a partner type of person. If the husband observes the newfound attention, he'll likely respond with a bit of jealousy and lavish more attention on the wife. This slight jealousy will also show in how he makes love to her. After all, he doesn't want to loose a successful partner does he?

As a wife, it is important to try to go back in your memory and identify why your husband chose to marry you. This assumes that you were chosen for reasons other than convenience or pregnancy.

If you were chosen because you are a source of inspiration, then return to the days when just a kind word from you would have him believe that he can conquer the world. Return to the days when you stroked his ego as no other woman could. Never let him forget, through your actions and words, that you were the first woman to see how brilliant, talented or special he is.

Whatever you do, don't make crazy statements like, "You owe me" or "You were nothing until you met me." A preferable statement would be: "I married you, because you were so proud and driven" or "I believed in you when we first married and I still do." Tell him how great he is at providing for his loved ones. Let him know that as a husband he's top shelf.

If you are a trophy wife, you should think about following the steps outlined for mistresses in staying desirable. Most trophy wives come along after the man has distinguished himself as a financial success and it is not uncommon that a trophy wife starts off as a mistress.

If you are a mistress, remind him once again through your actions and words that he still makes you tingle. Tell him how desirable he still is to you. Remind him of how, the first time you saw him, you got butterflies in your stomach. Stay away from phrases like "Do you still think I'm pretty?"

Also let him see you doing things to make yourself more desirable as a sex symbol. Take care of your nails, hair and figure. Stay up on the new sex crazes. Plan trips to sexy and erotic places, like strip clubs, Las Vegas and nude beaches. You can even arrange for a private dancer to come over and entertain the both of you, if you can't get away for a vacation. Whatever you do "keep sex alive" or you're dead.

As the slave, you must remember that it is your submissive presence that makes him feel like the all-powerful Oz. Even if you become extremely close to him, don't ever think that you are suddenly his partner or sexy mistress.

You are not. You are his slave, servant and employee. Sexually, you are his property to be taken at his will. To retain this position, you need to remind him that you are below him and submissive to him, that your destiny lies in his hands and that you accept this place because you have chosen such a wise man to lead, guide and dominate you.

The bottom line for all three women is to identify the reasons that you were chosen by this man, identify the position that you hold in his life and work hard to maintain those attributes and that particular place. Do not put your energy in displacing the other women unless you are getting A's in your own position.

I know of a very powerful and driven husband who married a very sexy but submissive slave type of woman. In the beginning, this worked out, but the man was highly ambitious, and it soon came to have its drawbacks.

He was unable to help her make the transition from the slave mentality to the wife mentality. Trying to get her to take her place as his partner proved very frustrating.

He soon found a solution by bonding with a very exceptional female coworker and removing the pressure from his wife to be anything other than who she was. He reversed the positions geographically by having his slave type at home and his wife type at work. The wife type at work helped him plan and achieve a very successful career and his slave type wife focused on keeping herself visually and sexually pleasing.

CHAPTER 18

IT'S NOT JUST SEX

It is helpful to understand that sex with each woman means something entirely different to the man. For example, sex with the wife, especially a wife who is highly competent and desirable as an asset in a man's life, indicates that he must be doing something right. Every man knows the stupid and selfish things he does. He should figure that, she still desires him and loves him because he's a great partner and never quits trying to provide for his family.

Sex with the mistress indicates to the man that he's attractive, successful and desirable. This may not be true, but he'll reach this conclusion based on the fact that he is married and he'll rationalize that there's no other reason she would want to be with him. He will garner her love and sexual favor because not only has he never quit trying but that he has actually succeeded in his endeavors.

This is the relationship that has bragging rights in the company of his male friends and counterparts. And the hotter she is the harder he brags.

Sex with the slave/servant/employee indicates, in his mind, that he has control and power and he is the one in charge. The man in this case may or may not be looking for a sexual relationship, but the difference in ranking and possibly class will reinforce his feeling of power and superiority. Not only has he tried but he has succeeded and now he has control over others.

Men have sex for all these reasons and more. So if it is the woman's intent to try and be all of these different women, then she will need to be keen enough and astute enough to identify which particular sexual need he has at a specific time. Once that need is identified, she will need to be flexible enough to switch roles from wife to mistress to slave. Good luck. This is more pressure than I would ever want to take on.

SEX AND THE WIFE

So, what is the wife's position sexually? This might be surprising, but the wife is the one primarily responsible for her husband's sexual satisfaction; whether she takes an active hands-on approach or she subcontracts it out to others.

It is unfortunate for her that sometimes sex with her husband will become a mundane chore, because of the lack of passion. However, this is part of her job description.

During the honeymoon and dating stages, the wife is the partner in sexual experimentation. Because most men don't marry sluts, the wife is expected to follow her husband's lead. This can be incredibly frustrating to a wife who has more experience than her husband, or a wife that has picked up new ideas from reading the vast amount of info contained in women's magazines.

Another challenge that the wife faces is the pedestal syndrome. Many men put their queens on a pedestal and, therefore, believe that sex with her should be sterile. If the wife desires treatment like a slut, she risks the possibility of being dethroned. My suggestion for those wives who want to come down from the pedestal is: Don't. Stay up there.

If you need something nasty and naughty to break up the monotony, try this: Do whatever you need to make yourself so sexually aroused that you are about ready to explode. Don't try to fondle him or get him in the mood with your touches unless he specifically told you he likes this. Once you are ready to blow, whisper in his ear, "I'm so sorry, husband, but when I think about how hard you work and all of the things that you provide for me, I get so wet that I can't stand it."

This tactic should work as long as there is a past history of sex in the marriage. Basically remember that men love to give their women orgasm. We love to know that what we do and who we are makes our women hot. The wife's challenge is to make sure that he knows that her sexual excitement is associated with his success as a provider and husband.

SEX AND THE MISTRESS

The mistress' place sexually, to be a new and exciting sexual pleasure. Since she'll more than likely have a sexual background, her experiences will usually have been very extensive.

As a pro-mistress, she will often introduce him to new ideas or possible first experiences. It is not unusual for successful men to know little to nothing about sex. You see most successful men have spent their years focused on their business endeavors and not sex. This is the time that the pro-mistress has spent her energy focusing on her business, which is sex. Even if the mistress plays submissive to the man, she may still be in charge every step of the way, telling him step by step what to do to her.

SEX AND THE SLAVE

With regard to the slave, the sexual practices that I'm most familiar with are derived from the lifestyle known as BDSM. An in depth look into the world of BDSM is beyond this book's scope, but here's a brief glossary of the terms for the purpose of better understanding the BDSM relationships:

BDSM: Bondage, Discipline, Sadism and Masochism. This is a generic term that derived from practices of fetishes which involve tying up, discipline and sexual satisfaction or arousal from inflicting and receiving pain. Originally it was know as just S&M.

Vanilla: Any lifestyle or sexuality not encompassed in the BDSM or sexual Fetish world.

Bondage: The act or art of tying up a partner or self for the sake of sexual arousal or satisfaction.

Discipline: 1) a way of life usually outlined with protocol and expectations. 2) A punishment or correction given for swaying from a particular protocol or failure to adhere to an instruction. The main objective is still sexual arousal or satisfaction.

Sadism: a term derived from a description of the activities enjoyed by the Marquee DeSade, the world's most renowned hedonist. It is the sexual arousal or satisfaction from inflicting pain.

Masochism: It is the sexual arousal or satisfaction from receiving pain.

Dominant: 1) an adjective describing the personality or behavior of a controlling or overbearing individual. 2) As a noun, it is a name or title given to the dominant person in a Dominant/submissive relationship

Submissive: 1) an adjective describing the personality or behavior of a passive or subservient individual. 2) As a noun, it is a name or title given to the submissive person in a Dominant/submissive relationship

Master: The person who has assumed control of another's life either through coercion or command in a Master/slave (M/S) relationship.

Slave: The person that has given up control of their life either voluntarily or involuntarily to another in a Master/slave (M/S) relationship.

Top: 1) as a verb it is being active or assertive in a sexual or BDSM encounter 2) As a noun, it is an individual who gets sexual arousal or satisfaction from being the active or assertive partner in a sexual or BDSM encounter.

Bottom: 1) as a verb it is being passive or submissive in a sexual or BDSM encounter 2) As a noun, it is an individual who gets sexual arousal or satisfaction from being the passive or submissive partner in a sexual or BDSM encounter.

Safe-word: A predetermined word that is used by the sub, slave or bottom to indicate that he or she has reached his/her pain or fear threshold. The Dominant or Top is to ease off or stop upon hearing the safe-word.

The position of the slave is to provide exercise for or to satisfy the sexual and nonsexual needs of a dominant partner. She is there to do anything and everything that his imagination can come up with. The sexual slave will have no limits on what she is willing to do to satisfy her man and it is this total submission that keeps him coming back for more. The sexual slave is usually the last stop of sexual experiences for most men. Anything after her is probably illegal.

MY DOGMA'S BETTER THAN YOURS

The BDSM world would have you believe that the honesty, love and devotion assigned in a Master/slave (M/S) or Dominant/submissive (D/S) relationship far surpasses that of their vanilla counterparts. In fact, if you bite on some of the rhetoric you'd begin to think that the whole idea of honor in marriage is total bullsh*t.

Yet if these claims were true, why are there proportionally just as many slaves looking for masters as there are women looking for husbands. If these claims really held weight, there would be no breakups in the BDSM community. The only thing that I can give to an M/s or D/s relationship is that the roles which each will play in the union are understood before hand.

This is, however, a generality. Many people involved in the BDSM world are only interested in sexual or sado-masochistic domination and submission. Get these same players outside the bedroom and they struggle for control and role definition, just like any couple.

YES SIR

The first time Michael heard the words "Yes Sir" roll of the tongue of a submissive he knew that he had entered a realm of unsurpassed devotion, or at least he thought he had. He hadn't been in the BDSM lifestyle very long but knew that he should have no trouble adapting to it. He had been to one BDSM club and witnessed a little play. From what he saw he figured it should be a piece of cake, rough sex with toys. Plus with his extensive background in martial arts he believed that learning to use the whips, floggers, crops and paddles would be a breeze. He surmised it should be no different than using a bamboo whip, nunchucks or any of the other martial arts weapons that he had been exposed to. Also, being trained in a strict karate dojo exposed Michael to a very traditional protocol. He was quite accustomed being addressed as Sir or Sensei and expected nothing less from the new submissive in his life.

They made arrangements to meet one Saturday afternoon at her place. "I want you wearing a red full length night gown when I get there" he commanded. "Yes sir," was the only reply he heard or needed to hear. He donned himself in all black all the way down to his black satin bikinis. He jumped into the car slapped in a disc of his favorite hardcore music and pushed off for a new adventure.

He saw the lines on the freeway whip by as he drove to her place in anticipation of what would unfold that day. They had only met one other time but he knew that she was ready to submit. He knew that she was ready to give her all to him and he was ready to claim that which would be his. He had once read that control is the ultimate aphrodisiac and now he understood exactly what was meant. As he pulled into the apartment complex Michael called her from his cell. He had already told her what he wanted her wearing and she ensured him that she would comply. Now his instructions were to unlock the front door and be kneeling behind it head down. She was to speak only when spoken to.

He commanded her every breath in that session and she was as responsive as a finely tuned sports car. Her body quaked from orgasm after orgasm. He was right. His martial arts experience gave him quick mastery of every toy and tool in the house. He was ever aware of how hard he would spank and whip her. He read her body language to insure that the pain he was delivering was being received by her as pleasure. She was a heavy player and worked without safe-words. The session was a combination of high intensity sex and BDSM ecstasy. He used her for his pleasure and was sure that he had brought her as much as she had brought him.

As they lay there panting and drenched she looked at him with those big beautiful eyes and said "Thank you Sir that was wonderful." Michael beamed with pride at how masterfully he had handled his first BDSM session. Then in a calm but confident voice she whispered "Now I need you to put your clothes on and get out. I have company coming."

The point is that understanding of roles in the bedroom does not necessarily constitute the same understanding outside the boudoir. Michael assumed that he would be given complete control of her from that point forward, that she'd be his slave. What she turned out to be was his first encounter with a sexual and BDSM bottom. My advice is that a bottom makes a great mistress, but as far as being a slave, I'd say throw her back and keep fishing.

CHAPTER 19

CHOOSE WISELY

I can't express enough the original reason for marriage, the building and retaining of wealth. And that only through the romanticizing of the wedding process do people have this desire to marry for love. The wedding has always been a source of celebration, but that original celebration was not about love, but rather the family of the bride celebrating the fact that they would not have to take care of her for the rest of their lives.

It is this change in reasons for getting married that has brought so much divorce to Western civilization. I would like to see a day when both parties make the decision to marry for social-economic reasons in addition to love or passion. There would be fewer single-parent homes and more opportunity and education for the children.

After the passion is gone, if no other basis for the marriage exists, soon the marriage will be gone, too.

Marriage is a legally binding institution first of all and a relationship second. The sad fact is that we are very rarely reminded of this legal bond until it is time to get a divorce.

We are very rarely reminded about the power of the institution of marriage itself. We are rarely reminded that two people working together for a common goal are more apt to reach it than one person, toiling alone.

Only at the time of a divorce are we reminded that a marriage really can exist without love or passion. We are reminded that it is only a choice to break up the institution, because of a lack of either. Had the marriage come about for social-economic reasons in addition to love or passion, it would probably make more sense to stay together than to divorce.

Isn't it amazing that, out of the three relationships (the wife, the mistress and the slave), that the mistress relationship is the only one not governed by law? Obviously, the marriage is governed by laws of community property and the illegality of taking on more than one wife or husband. The slave/servant relationship is also governed by labor, sexual harassment and anti-slavery laws. So, the only relationship not governed by the law is the one based on love, sex and passion, the mistress relationship. This being said if a man chooses the wrong woman for a position or if a woman chooses to occupy a position that is not suited for her, then there is a very good chance that the couple will end in court.

I leave you with this: Men, choose wisely the women that will hold these positions in your life. A wrong choice can leave everyone in its wake devastated. And women choose just as carefully the position that you wish to hold in a man's life. And if you desire to hold all three, expect a life forever changing, because the only constant in man and the universe is change.